IN THE MIND OF A FEMALE SERIAL KILLER

IN THE MIND OF A FEMALE SERIAL KILLER

Stephen Jakobi

PEN & SWORD HISTORY

First published in Great Britain in 2017 by
Pen & Sword History
an imprint of
Pen & Sword Books Ltd
47 Church Street
Barnsley
South Yorkshire
S70 2AS

Copyright © Stephen Jakobi, 2017

ISBN 9781526709714

Printed and bound in the UK by CPI Group (UK) Ltd,
Croydon, CRO 4YY

Pen & Sword Books Ltd incorporates the Imprints of Pen & Sword
Archaeology, Atlas, Aviation, Battleground, Discovery, Family
History, History, Maritime, Military, Naval, Politics, Railways,
Select, Transport, True Crime, Fiction, Frontline Books, Leo
Cooper, Praetorian Press, Seaforth Publishing, Wharncliffe and
White Owl.

For a complete list of Pen & Sword titles please contact
PEN & SWORD BOOKS LIMITED
47 Church Street, Barnsley, South Yorkshire, S70 2AS, England
E-mail: enquiries@pen-and-sword.co.uk
Website: www.pen-and-sword.co.uk

Contents

Preface

During six short weeks that the most successful female serial killer in modern British history was in the service of Mr Gardner, a total of three dogs, one cat, one parrot, twelve canaries and linnets, and some goldfish died very mysteriously.

She was in service of Mr Brown a fortnight, during which time the cat, a canary, a linnet and some goldfish died, and the parrot was thought to be dying. Mr Judd, a bird fancier, was called in to see it, and he was of the opinion that its neck had been pinched, it being swollen at the time.

In September 1870, she was in the service of Mr Thomas for about a month, and while there, a fowl and three canaries died mysteriously. The fowl was found behind some wood where it could not have reached without having being placed there. All the live animals at the house had died.

During the three days she was in the service of Mrs Beer, a cat and a canary both died mysteriously.

The grand total of three dogs, three cats, at least seventeen canaries and linnets, numerous goldfish, one parrot and a fowl had been killed over a two-year period, ending in April 1871 when she was brought to book. She had only been in employment for a total of four months.

In these four households, she also committed four murders of babies and toddlers (the oldest nearly 3) and two attempted murders of older children. Agnes Norman was 13 years old when she started her killing spree and 15 when it ended. She was only convicted of one attempted murder.

Introduction

On Thursday, 13 July 1955, Ruth Ellis was executed. For me, this led to a lifelong crusade against capital punishment and my eventual career as an international criminal defence lawyer. It was not until after retirement that I could study other incidents of mistreatment of women by the reprieve system. I did not consider that notorious miscarriage of justice in the 1920s, the execution of Edith Thompson, since so much has already been written about it. The same applied to Ruth Ellis. A little-known case, battered wife Emily Swann, who was executed at the beginning of the twentieth century, had recently been studied by Dr Anette Ballinger[1]. There did not seem any other serious miscarriages of justice in the twentieth century, but I went through the other Home Office files of the late nineteenth and twentieth centuries that are held in the National Archives at Kew[2].

These Home Office files, once opened to the public, must be the first source of information about the condemned. For over 100 years, the final decision on a reprieve was made by the Home Secretary. In the 1920s, a retired Permanent Secretary to the Home Office wrote about the procedures followed after a death sentence has been pronounced.[3]

> When any prisoner is sentenced to death, this is immediately reported to the Home Office by the Governor of the prison. The Judge also writes to the Home Secretary, forwarding a copy of his notes of the evidence and reporting any recommendation of the jury. The Judge sometimes states at once his own opinion on the case but more frequently waits before expressing his views until the prisoner's appeal has been heard or the Home Office has asked for them. In most cases petitions are received from the prisoner's solicitor or his friends. In any case that has excited much public attention, whatever its merits, petitions from the public pour in in large numbers. But whether there are any petitions or not, minute enquiries are made through the police and otherwise into the prisoner's history and character into all circumstances which may throw light on the motive the murder and of an any uncertain features in the crime … In most cases the Home Secretary's final

decision is not announced until three days before the date fixed for the execution. These files contain all the relevant information about the condemned known to the authorities at the time.

This procedure, with the Home Office 'death files' it gave rise to, commenced in the 1850s and was to be continued, virtually unchanged, until the abolition of capital punishment in the 1960s. Their contents used to be subject to 100 years' burial as Official Secrets before being opened to the public, but a recent relaxation has made files over 70 years old accessible. This batch included the case of Louie Calvert, a little-known serial killer of the 1920s. Her death file would otherwise have remained locked away for another decade.

This led to my discovery of an exercise book, her remarkable 5,000-word autobiography written in the condemned cell at Strangeways, Manchester, a few days before her execution[4]. But how true was it?

My knowledge of legal procedure had benefits. The penultimate stage in the preparation of the case for trial is where the prosecutor considers all the witness statements and documents, before telling the police to warn those whom he considers are central to the case to be available for the trial. There is a discard pile of witness statements involving inadmissible evidence, irrelevancies to the main theme of the prosecution case, and other superfluous material. The whole of the evidence, used or unused, is to be found in the prosecutor's papers that were part of the death file. The only information the police really had about the early days of Calvert's life are to be found in Sister Edith's statement to the police. The course of the relationship between Calvert and Mrs Waterhouse, her final victim, is to be found in the statement of the bookseller who sent her to the police. Neither of them gave evidence in public.

Calvert's criminal record comprised mainly petty thefts in petty sessions. She was sent to the West Riding quarter sessions held in Leeds twice, once so that she could be sent for borstal training, and ten years later because the housebreaking offence was so serious the magistrates could not deal with it. Fortunately, the procedure involved in sending a case for trial to quarter sessions meant that the quarter sessions' records include the sworn witness statements given before the magistrates. There was no trial as such, since, inevitably, Calvert pleaded guilty. Otherwise she appeared in the magistrates' courts of Ossett, Dewsbury, Leeds, and once in Bradford. It was necessary to either travel to local museums, who held the archives of such minor trials as were available, or employ researchers.

I researched local records in Leeds and Wakefield with the help of Calvert's great-niece, Susan Holt, who had grown up in Calvert's home town of Ossett, West Yorkshire. It was Holt who supplied me with the revealing family photographs mutilated by her grandmother, Calvert's sister Edith. Unfortunately, the archives are incomplete. I was forced to rely on local newspapers of the time (*Ossett Observer, Dewsbury Recorder*) for the petty sessions details. I did manage to discover, however, that in the 1920s, journalists used shorthand, and where it was possible to compare the clerk's notes with the report in the local paper, the accounts were virtually identical. For information on spells in prison and date of release, the prison governor's diary, known as the prison calendar, is the best source of information. With the aid of ancestry.com[5] and Internet search engines, I discovered much of the complex truth.

Were there similar cases?

I returned to Kew and read through the remaining files. I found two other interesting cases of last-minute confessions. One of them was made by Kate Webster, the notorious Richmond killer who cut up and boiled her mistress's body in 1879, before disposing of most of it in the River Thames – the head was found buried in Sir David Attenborough's orchard in 2010. Kate Webster's method of victim disposal, and her extraordinary behaviour after the murder, made her so notorious that fifty years later she was the subject of a volume in the *Notable British Trials* series[6].

The other was that of the last of the 'baby farmers', Mrs Willis. In 1907, the day before her execution, she 'confessed' to her solicitor that, although she had been arrested, tried and sentenced under the name of Leslie James, her name was really Rhoda Willis, and she had been born Rhoda Lascelles to a well-to-do family in Sunderland. Mrs Willis remains an enigma as her final story to her lawyer was false. Whatever her birth name might have been, it was not Rhoda, and she married Mr Willis twice in different parts of the country. Researchers in Sunderland and Cardiff failed to give answers.

I had more or less completed the preparation of this book when I came across the case of Agnes Norman. Very little about this enigmatic woman has ever appeared in public. Never the subject of a death file, it is an extraordinary saga for which the only relevant archives are misleading press cuttings, verbatim records of two trials, and a Scotland Yard file.

What surprised me in all my investigations was the previous lack of interest in the old court records. Wherever I went I had to wash my hands after examining them. As a result, I have been able to discover considerable new material about these serial killers.

It includes the only photograph, hitherto unpublished, of Louie Calvert, contemporary drawings, also unpublished since the trial, of Mrs Willis, and the probable solution to three unsolved murders and the explanation of one of the key puzzles in the 'Thames Torso' murders.

In this book, I attempted to write the biographies of four notorious murderesses from background and birth to grave. I believe I have succeeded in answering the fundamental questions about their crimes and trials. However, each of their stories has a chapter entitled 'The problem with ...', dealing with researching the gaps in their personal lives. The story of Agnes Norman ends with her marriage, while the story of Emma Willis starts with hers.

To retain character and authenticity, the writings of the individuals who feature in this publication have been transcribed entirely untouched.

PART 1
Agnes Norman

Timeline

1856
Born in Clipston, Northamptonshire.

1860
Moves to London.

1869

January	Enters service of Ralf Milner.
10 February	Death of baby Thomas Milner.
24 February	Death of infant Amelia.

1870

20 April	Enters service of Mr Gardner.
1 May	Death of baby John Stuart Taylor.
18 May	Death of infant James Gardner.
August	Enters service of Mr Brown, staying a fortnight. Attempted murder of 10-year-old Charles Parfitt.
September	In the service of Mr Thomas.

1871

5 April	Enters service of Mr Beer.
7 April	Death of infant Jesse Jane Beer.
11 April	Inquest on Jesse Jane Beer.
28 April	Arrested on charge of murdering Jesse Jane Beer. Taken before the magistrates at Lambeth Police Court on the 29th.
10 July	The trials at the old Bailey. 1. Murder of Jesse Jane Beer: verdict, not guilty. 2. Attempted murder of Charles Parfitt. Verdict, guilty. Sentenced to ten years in prison.

1871–1880
Imprisonment in Marshalsea, Woking and Manchester prisons.

1880

29 July	Married William Henry Cowlan.

1. What We Know About Her Life

> When Adam delved and Eve span who was then the gentle
> man?
> Radical priest, John Ball, 1381 revolt.

Agnes Norman was born in 1856, the eldest daughter of Joseph Norman, a bootmaker living in Clipston, Northamptonshire, and his wife Elizabeth. The family moved to London in 1860. In 1869, she commenced the two-year killing spree outlined in the prologue. In 1871, she was tried on two separate offences, receiving a prison sentence of ten years. On her release in 1881, she married William Henry Cowlan, before disappearing from records.

The Northampton village of Clipston, according to the 1851 census, had 800 inhabitants, and would have been typical of similar agricultural villages in middle England. However, it was part of the Northampton–Bedford–North Buckinghamshire area that specialized in growing flax and lace making. While Adam delved, there were 140 agricultural labourers and 20 self-employed farmers with small holdings. Eve was a 'lace runner'. Lace running was a cottage industry that employed the wives and daughters of the agricultural labourers in piecework embroidery of patterns on lace. There were seventy-five lace runners in the village, typically very young, the usual age being 10 or 11, but some were as young as 5.

The other unusual activity for a small village was the industrial scale of boot- and shoe-making. The village had a baker, a blacksmith, a carpenter and a bricklayer, but it had fifteen shoemakers. Two of these were masters employing a journeyman and apprentices, the rest independent craftsmen. The village was a full day's journey from Northampton, the centre of England's boot- and shoe-making trade, causing one to wonder whether the village output was sent to Northampton for sale.

Joseph Norman, the son of an agricultural labourer, appears in the 1851 census as a shoemaker. In 1853, he married Elizabeth Buttin, only daughter of a smallholding farmer in a neighbouring village. She was three years his senior. Did the father have anything to do with his apprenticeship?

Agnes Norman was born in Clipston in 1856, the eldest daughter of Joseph and Elizabeth. She had two elder brothers, George, born in 1852, and Walter, born the same year she was, but not a twin. In 1860, Joseph moved to the Saint Sepulchre area of Clerkenwell, where siblings William (1861), Mary (1864), Anne (1868), Joseph (1869), and twins Naomi and Emily (1870) were born.

At Norman's second trial, it was mentioned that she had confided to a friend that she did not like children. One can picture her relief at leaving home in 1869–70 where she was probably responsible for looking after five siblings under the age of six.

On conviction, she was sent to Marshalsea Prison, a holding prison for young females, before being transferred a few months later to Woking Prison, then the newly opened main prison for females in England. She was the youngest prisoner when she arrived and, incidentally, a contemporary of Kate Webster.

At some stage, she was transferred to Manchester, a young female offenders' unit at the time, and from there, on release, married William Henry Cowlan, the son of a musical-instrument maker who lived close by her family home in Lambeth. The Normans and the Cowlans were extremely close. In 1878, Catherine Cowlan, born in the same year as Agnes Norman, and presumably a personal friend, married her elder brother Walter. Norman therefore married her brother-in-law, Catherine's younger brother. Walter was one of the witnesses. William died in St Thomas's Hospital on 28 August 1890, his residence being given as his father's home Newington Butts. They had no children. Norman presumably changed her name and there would appear to be no later public record about her.

2. The Suspicions of Detective Sergeant Mullard

The usual venue of a coroner's court in England during these times was a local tavern. The inquest on Jessie Jane Beer, aged 14 months, conducted in April 1871 before Mr Carter, the coroner for East Surrey, was held at the King and Queen tavern, Newington Butts. It would have passed virtually unnoticed had it not been for the sensational evidence of Detective Sergeant Henry Mullard, attached to L Division of the Metropolitan Police. His evidence concerned the actions and antecedents of the child's nursemaid, Agnes Norman. There is an extraordinary parallel to the Constance Kent case. The nursemaid to that household, Elizabeth Gough, was initially arrested but then released.

It is not known how the activities of Agnes Norman came to the attention of Mr Mullard. The usual procedure in the late-nineteenth century was one in which the coroner's officer, a serving or retired police officer, would perform the initial investigation. It could have been through William White from the coroner's office, or Mr Beer, the child's father, that the Lambeth police became involved.

Jesse Beer died on Tuesday, 7 April 1871. In the six days between her death and the following Monday, 13 April, when the inquest took place, Sergeant Mullard's investigations had been completed. His evidence was ready for court. In only four working days, he had managed to locate and interview a score of relevant witnesses, including a number of local doctors, putting together what eventually turned out to be a literally incredible story.

Subsequent events made it clear that the inquest, and the way it was conducted by the coroner, left both Sergeant Mullard and the child's father profoundly dissatisfied with the result. Afterwards, both went to the press.

It was not until 19 April, six days after the inquest, that a national newspaper, *The Morning Advertiser*, started a public outcry over the activities of Agnes Norman[1]. The article clearly aimed for sensationalism. It began:

'Some circumstances which read like a horrible tale of Eastern Thugee, or some morbid conception of an opium eater, are stated in the report of an enquiry before Mr Carter coroner for East Surrey on Monday last'.

It cited the evidence of Mr Beer about his infant daughter Jesse and her death, and the evidence of the surgeon that she been suffocated, adding that the servant girl had been employed by the Beers for only three days before the event. It said that Mr Mullard, detective officer, stated a series of facts about her, 'so starkly is almost to exceed the bare possibility of belief, he said, 'several children had expired under similar circumstances.'

The article went into some detail, without disclosing names of the families or children concerned. It continued:

> Now, we do not wish for one moment to assert our belief in this category of horrors. In the last instance the child might have fallen out of bed and been suffocated between the bed and the wall. Such things do occur. But either Detective Sgt Mullard has been listening to a number of romances and cruel groundless scandals, all the tragic suggestiveness of his story is of a nature to curdle the blood with horror and take away the breath. We are bound to – and heaven knows we wish to – believe that the jury had good reason for being impressed with the girls innocence, since they returned a verdict that Mr and Mrs Beers child 'died from suffocation accidentally caused' but if so where is Detective Sgt Mullard's judgement and discretion?

The article went on to make the obvious point:

> The father professed himself dissatisfied; and well he
> might, under the circumstances; and so are we, in one
> sense. It would have been just towards the girl – and not
> unjust, as the coroner said it would be, in his opinion –
> to examine the witnesses in court who could offer direct
> evidence concerning these grave imputations.

The article ended:

'As the matter stands conjecture is rife. The unfortunate and
bereaved father has declared that the matter shall not rest there;
and we think for the sake of the girl, if she be innocent, who rests
under such suspicions, and for the public satisfaction that it is as
well it should not'.

On Wednesday, 22 April, three days later, the *London Evening
Standard* published a much longer article about the affair. This one
commenced:

> A strange rumour ran through the town a fortnight ago
> to the effect that the nursemaid had been detected whose
> mania was the destruction of the children committed to
> her charge. An inquest was then opened at Newington
> Butts on the body of an infant, one year and two months
> old, who had unquestionably come by its death under
> very extraordinary and even startling circumstances ... We
> are most anxious not to give the mystery, for that there
> is a mystery will soon be seen, any prejudicial colouring
> whatsoever it may be as well, therefore, to quote, without
> comment, a short colloquy which, at this point, took place
> between the representative of the law and the parent of
> the dead infant. The father of the deceased here said he
> had witnesses present who could give a history of the girl
> Norman.
>
> The Coroner: 'have you any witnesses who can say that
> this girl has murdered your child?'
>
> Mr Beer: 'I am unable to say that, but I should like
> these persons to be examined.'
>
> The Coroner: 'I do not think I should be doing justice
> to this girl if I examine them.'
>
> Mr Beer: 'if a verdict is given without, I shall think it
> very unfair.'
>
> Whereupon a statement was made (by the coroner)
> of so singular a character that the inexplicable verdict
> subsequently given 'that the deceased died of suffocation

accidentally caused' does not dispose of it at all. (He said) there was no more proof of accident than there was of violence, and of violence there was not unless we attach importance to the marks on the lips and even with respect to then it was not sought to be shown that any particular individual was implicated.'

But the statement, we repeat, was made, and made by Detective Sgt Mullard an officer attached to the Kennington Lane police station. We desire to take it at not one iota more than it is strictly worth, or maybe worth, after a commentary to it has been supplied. It may betray the existence of a terrible morbid instinct, impossible to comprehend; it may represent no more than a series of marvellous coincidences or it may be an exaggeration though that is not likely.

The *London Evening Standard* then demands, for the sake of the girl herself, a thorough scrutiny into a set of allegations so alarming to society is peremptorily demanded:

When the inquest was first opened the report floated about with respect to this nursemaid that when previously engaged in gentleman's families, no fewer than four children in her charge had died mysteriously. It was to ascertain the truth or falsehood this assertion the silent and secret detective sagacity was employed. We repeat, boldly, the evidence given by Sgt Mullard after completing his researches, clearly not less on the girl's behalf than that of the public that the horrible doubts thus suggested must be set at rest in one way or another.

The other half of the article goes into considerable detail, without naming the names of the families involved the article and concluded:

… but the truth though, at all events, to be traced home; for the detective's version of the story is enough to chill the blood of every mother in the land who employs a nursemaid. Everyone must be anxious that a part, at least, of the mystery should be dispelled or proved to have been of an innocent nature.

A grieving parent backed by a thwarted detective, had started a public outcry.

3. The Reinvestigation

The commissioner's office at Scotland Yard had reacted quickly to the *Morning Advertiser*'s article. A file on Agnes Norman was opened immediately.[1]

By this time, the Metropolitan Police district was an area covering about a ten-mile radius from Charing Cross, comprising twenty police divisions. The relevant police division was 'L - Lambeth'. Each division was headed by a superintendent with four inspectors and sixteen sergeants working for him. The commissioner initialled an order to his local superintendent, 'Mr Williamson – have careful enquiry made into the article referring to Detective Sgt Mullard.' Evidently Mr Williamson had ordered one of his inspectors to conduct the investigation.

On 28 April, the inspector's handwritten report was available for the commissioner:

Metropolitan police office, Scotland Yard
28 April 1871

I beg to report with reference to the attached newspaper extracts respecting the statement of Detective Sgt Mullard L division, as to the antecedents of Agnes Norman, who was a servant to John William Beer 58, Newington Butts, when his child Jesse Jane Beer died mysteriously of suffocation; that I have made careful enquiry into the matter, and found that in January 1869 she was in the service of Ralph Milner 19 Park Road Kennington whom I have seen, and he stated that she entered his service without a character and remained about two months. Soon after she came the baby Thomas Milner, 10 months old, was found to have a severely bruised arm which got well in about five weeks, and his elder son Alfred, aged eight years told him that Agnes let the baby fall off the table, and gave him a halfpenny not to say anything about it, and on 10 February 1869 he went out at 2 PM leaving Agnes Norman in charge of his four children and on his return at 4:30 PM the youngest child Thomas was dead, – this child was not particularly unwell at the time, but it had been ill from teething, and had had convulsions during the previous week, and that Dr Nott, Lucas Road Kennington, had attended the child and was called in at its death, but he refused to give a certificate of the cause

of its dying, an inquest was then held upon the body
by J Carter Esq coroner, when a verdict of natural death
[a fit in dentition] was returned. Agnes Norman gave
evidence on this occasion and on 24 February 1869 she
was left in charge of his three children at 10:30 AM and on
his return at 10 PM he found that his child Amelia aged
two years and 10 months had died during the day she
was a rather delicate child and powders were obtained for
her of Mr Steedman, chemist, Walworth Road a few days
previous to her death. Dr Nott, Lucas Road Kennington
refused to give a certificate of the cause of death.

William Smith coroner's officer came and took the
particulars of the case but no inquest was held. He had no
suspicion at the time against Agnes Norman but shortly
after the death of the second child she was sent upstairs
at 9:30 PM to put his son Arthur age 6 years to bed, and
when she came down he was heard to groan and on his
going upstairs he found the child insensible. A Surgeon
was sent for a powder was given to him and he recovered
consciousness at 2 AM and when he got up in the morning
he appeared much better and stated that Agnes had bought
the ghost to him last night and he was afraid of her and did
not want to sleep in the room with her again –

The Mother of the Children Elizabeth Milner
corroborated the above statement, and further stated that
after her son 'Arthur' was found insensible, he told her that
Agnes Norman put his sister 'Amelia' into the wardrobe,
and gave him a halfpenny not to say anything about it
and that her son 'Alfred' age 8 years, stated that he asked
Agnes where his sister was, and she said she was in bed, he
then went to her bed there was only a pillow in it. He then
told her she was not there, when she went to the closed
cupboard and took her out of it, and laid her upon the floor,
and that she appeared very pale, and that she gave him and
his brother a halfpenny each not to say what she had done.

Mrs Milner thinks that the oldest boy can give a clear
account of the matter, and could be well relied upon for
his truthfulness, but the father says that he is very excitable
and that he does not think he could give any constant
particulars of the servant having placed the child and the
wardrobe, and the present he declines to allow the boy to
be examined about it, as he thinks it would frighten him,
Mrs Milner told the mother of Agnes Norman what the
boys had said, and discharged her from her service –

Mrs Hodson 18 pack road Kennington states that on 10 February 1869 at 3 ½ p.m. Agnes Norman called her to look at the baby Thomas Milner whom she stated was very cold, and on her entering she found the child dead, she sent for Dr Nott who said the child had been dead some time. She attended before the Coroner and gave her evidence, and that 3 ½ p.m. 24th of February 1869 Agnes Norman called her in again and said the little girl Amelia appeared to be dead she went in and found the child undressed and in bed, quite dead, she asked the servant how it was she came to undress the child and put her to bed at that time of the day and she made no answer and appeared to treat the matter very lightly – as the time of the day when she came to her was just the same on each occasion, she had suspicion that something was wrong, and she took possession of some sausages and water which were left from the dinner of the children and gave them to the Coroner's Officer –

I have seen Dr Nott and he stated that he could not recollect anything of the circumstances of the treatment and deaths of the children, as it was so long ago.

About 20 April 1870 Agnes Norman entered the service of Mr Gardner 170 Stockwell Park Road, as nursemaid and on 1 May Mrs Taylor 56 Arthur Road Brixton went there on a visit and took her baby John Stuart Taylor aged five months with her and she states that the baby was in good health, that at 8 20 p.m. she took it upstairs and laid it on to its side in a bed in the nursery in which Agnes Norman was, and covered it up to the shoulders and left it there until 10:40 PM when she went upstairs to put her clothes on to go home and then found the child in about the same position in the bed as when she left it, but it was quite dead, Dr Pocock Brixton Road was called in and he stated that the child had been dead an hour. An inquest was held before W Carter Esq Coroner and a verdict of natural death due to spasms of the Glottis was returned. Agnes Norman gave evidence at this inquest.

On the 18th May 1870 Mr and Mrs Gardner went out at 8 ¼ p.m. and left their infant child James Alexander Gardner age 14 months in bed in charge of Agnes Norman at 8 ½ p.m. it cried, and as she was downstairs she went up to it and as she did not come down again shortly after the Cook went up to the nursery and found her kneeling down by her bedside with her head upon her arm as though she was asleep she roused her up, she then went downstairs and was soon followed by her, and at 9 PM they both went up into the nursery again found the baby dead. Dr Pocock Brixton Road was called in and he stated that he thought the baby had died of convulsions. Dr Swallow Kennington Park Road had however attended the child for 12 months and he gave a certificate that the child died of convulsions. He informed me that he was not at all surprised at its dying suddenly in there, as the child was very weak and sickly –

During the six weeks Agnes Norman was in the service of Mr Gardner three dogs a cat a parrot 12 canaries and linnets and some goldfish died very mysteriously.

In August 1870 Agnes Norman entered the service of Mr Brown 19 Temple Street St George's Road and had leave one day to go to the Crystal Palace to sleep at home that night. She came to Mr Brown's at 7:30 AM and was let in by Elizabeth Parfitt she went upstairs to the bedroom in which Charles Parfitt aged 10 years was sleeping to take off her bonnet. Directly afterwards the little boy was heard to call for his aunt she ran upstairs and found him crying and upon her asking him what was the matter he stated he felt as if the being suffocated, and when he awoke he found that Agnes Norman had one hand over his mouth and the other on his throat so that he could not breathe and when he screamed out she gave him a sweet not to say anything of it. She was present when he made the statement and said you wicked boy how could you say so you know I was at the mirror. The sweet was taken from his mouth by his aunt.

She was in service of Mr Brown's a fortnight, during which time, the cat, a canary, a linnet and some goldfish died and the parrot was thought to be dying. Mr Judd a bird fancier was called in to see it, and he was of the opinion that its neck had been pinched, it being swollen at the time.

I have seen the boy Charles Parfitt who is at school at Bracknell and he adheres to his mother's statement as to her having her hand over his mouth and on his throat when he awoke, and that he felt suffocating, and was very ill after it, but he appears to be a very timid boy and it was with difficulty that I could get answers to questions from him, and his friends think that he would be easily puzzled by cross questions and almost made to say anything.

About September last Agnes Norman was in the service of Mr Thomas 37 Carter Street Walworth for about a month, and while there a fowl and three canaries died mysteriously. The fowl was found behind some wood where it could not have got without being placed there. All the live animals at the house died.

On 5 April 1871 she entered the service of John William Beer 58 Newington Butts and on the seventh instant Mr and Mrs Beer went out at 3 ½ p.m. and left their three children in her charge, and on returning home at 12 ½ a.m. she was found asleep in front of the fire. Soon after their return one of the children appeared to fall out of bed. Mr Beer went upstairs to see what was the matter, and found one of his sons on the floor crying and wondered why the baby did not wake. He felt across the bed and found his child Jesse Jane Beer age 14 months dead. She was lying on her back with the head and part of the body uncovered, Dr Williams Walworth Road was called in, and he stated that the child had died of suffocation. Two marks were on the lower lip as if it had been pressed against the two upper teeth the child was very strong and healthy, and could get out of bed and walk.

I have seen Dr Lees 112 Walworth Road, who made the Post Mortem examination of the body, and he is of the opinion that something must have been pressed upon the mouth of the child till after life was extinct, and that he does not think it possible that suffocation could be caused by the child lying its mouth upon its hand, or against the wall or any hard substance sufficient to cause the marks on the lip, as the nose and chin would protect it from suffocation under such circumstances, and if it had been suffocated by anything soft he did not think such marks would appear upon the lip.

Sarah Millbank servant at 35 lower Kennington Lane, has also been seen and she stated that about 4 PM 7th instant she met Agnes Norman carrying Mrs Beers child from Kennington Park and she said the baby looks unwell, when she (Norman) said it had fits and on the Sunday after the child died she again met up, and asked what the shutters were up for when she said the baby is dead. It died at 6 ½ p.m. of fits. When the Father and Mother came home the boy fell out of bed and the father went upstairs and picked him up and found the baby dead. The Mother then ran upstairs and they called me to them but

I did not care to go in case they might say I had done something to it

The child had never had fits. She told Mrs Beer that she saw it all right at 10:30 PM she therefore for some reason told the force put to Sarah Milbank. During the three days she was in the service of Mrs Beer a cat and canary died mysteriously.

James Jay Inspector

Mr Williamson appended a note:

'It appears to me that there is enough evidence to arrest the girl on a charge of murdering Jesse Jane Beer and I would beg to suggest this course be adopted. Fred Williamson superintendent 28th April'.

The commissioner initialled the note 'approved'.

In the margin, at the head of the Detective Officer's Special Report Form, is the note, 'submit to Col Henderson'. Below that is the direction, 'lay these papers before the solicitor Mr Treadway when this case is before him'. Initialled 1 May.

Meanwhile, the public concern about the behaviour of Norman, and the coroner and his jury, had been strengthened by a letter written by two of the doctors on 27 April, published in the *Evening Standard* on the 28th:

Sir

We again notice in your issue of this morning that you call attention to the inquest held upon the child Jesse Jane Beer, and as our names have been brought before the public in connection with the matter we are exceedingly anxious that it should sifted, not only on our own account, but that of the girl Norman. We should be obliged, therefore, if you would allow us to call attention to the verdict of the … Jury … In defiance of the evidence of Dr Lees of inspector Mullard it will be remembered … That the evidence of Dr Lees … That the child's death was caused by suffocation, but he was unable to stay by what means the suffocation was caused.

This, we submit, by itself, should have prevented a jury who knew anything of the caution necessary for a man of Dr Lee's profession closing the matter by the summary means of a verdict of 'accidental death.'

But we submit further that the statement made by Sgt. Mullard … Makes out a very strong prima facie case against the girl. The facts then detailed – Viz. the children under her care have died in suspicious and nearly similar circumstances within the last 12 months, that cases have occurred of children being found, if not dead, almost at death's door, and that one child declares that he awoke upon one occasion and found the girl's hand upon his mouth and the other on his stomach and that he was afterwards bribed by the girl to say nothing of this occurrence, were sufficient, we submit, to have enabled and made it the duty of the jury to have investigated the case more fully, or to have referred it to another tribunal, or, at least, by returning an open verdict, to avoid the responsibility of closing the enquiry in a summary matter. It will be easily supposed that had they adopted the first or second course much more evidence would have been forthcoming and could be given in the summary of facts tendered to the inquest.

As we are dissatisfied, for the reasons you stated, with the finding of the jury, we feel bound to bring this matter before the public. Thanking you for having given publicity to the matter-we are Sir yours et cetera.

John Taylor Brixton
James P Gardner Stockwell

The letter was supported by a lengthy editorial on 29 April:

The circumstances associated with the death of the infant Jesse Jane Beer, already reported and commented upon in our columns, have received additional elucidation from an authoritative letter which we published yesterday these, responsibly stated, render it impossible that the case should be smothered out of public sight ... the entire story, and its effect, unless the secret is explained, will be felt in every nursery – in every family – throughout England, innocence of suspicion and alarm.

[The lengthy article continues to regurgitate the 'facts' as then surmised by the *Evening Standard*]

It concludes:

Have parents to live in the presence of a nameless terror, when their children might be imagined sleeping safely under their own roofs? Or are coroners to slam the door in the face of enquiries which they are appointed and paid to conduct so far as a glimpse of light is left for them to follow?

Society has been terrified by these revelations, and has a right to insist that the sudden and successive deaths, following rapidly, of so many infants in charge of one girl, in different nurseries should be more satisfactorily explained.

A police note attached to a copy of the article emphasizes the panic that the press campaign had created in Scotland Yard: 'Mr Williamson have you ascertained anything of the truth of this story?'

4. The Criminal Proceedings

On 1 May, the inspector reported that he had arrested Agnes Norman upon suspicion of murdering Jesse Jane Beer on 28April. She was taken before the magistrate at Lambeth Police Court on the 29th and remanded to 6 May. A note to his report by Superintendent Williamson states,[1] 'As this is a case of considerable importance and requires the evidence of the witnesses to be very carefully brought out, I beg to recommend that legal aid be employed.' Normally in a police court, the police would handle the prosecution.

A note on the file, dated 2 May, is from the Home Office, granting legal aid for the prosecutors.

Although the press gave lip service to the notion that it was vital to the girl to have the opportunity to clear her name, at the time she would have had no opportunity to give evidence in criminal proceedings. The accused was not allowed to give evidence until the law was changed in the 1880s. Accordingly, the real target of publicity and press was the conduct of the coroner. The first of the subsequent trials was, in effect, to appeal against the coroner's direction in the matter of Jesse Jane Beer.

In the trial for murder of Jesse Jane Beer on 10 July 1871,[2] the prosecution was headed by Harry Bodkin Poland, Treasury Counsel. In his opening address to the jury, he indicated that he would produce evidence as to the prisoner's disposition to commit crime. The judge intervened to state that he wished to consider whether evidence of a tendency or habit to commit crimes could not be given, nor evidence that animals died during the time the prisoner was in the service of various people as a domestic servant. After consulting the Lord Chief Justice and another senior judge, the judge said, 'The learned judges to whom I consulted are of opinion that such evidence must be excluded. As to the cases of unaccountable death of children under her care I shall admit that evidence and reserve the point.'

This therefore virtually upheld the coroner's view of the applicable law at the inquest.

JOHN WILLIAM BEER. I lived at 58 Newington Butts at the time of this occurrence. I am a dealer in jewellery and on 4 April, 1870, the prisoner came into my service as a general servant, to look after my children. I had three children, Arthur Samuel, 8 years; Alfred James, three years, and the deceased, 15 months the day she was buried. The prisoner was in my service one week. On 7th April I and my wife went out at about 2.45 in the afternoon, leaving the prisoner in charge of my children. She was the only servant. They were in perfect health, the deceased as well, she never had any illness in her life. We returned at 11:45 at night we went together into the sitting room, where the prisoner was apparently asleep. There was a very large fire. She sat close to the fire, in an armchair. She woke up by our entering the room. None of the children were in the room with her. I believe my wife spoke to her about the children. She said they were quite well. After I'd been in the room a few minutes I heard screaming from one of my children upstairs. It was usual for the children's bedroom to be locked after they'd gone to bed. I had several lodgers in the house. The key was kept in the sitting room. The bedroom was over the sitting room. We occupied the shop, sitting room and bedroom over it. The bedroom was five or six steps from the ground. The sitting room and shop were on the ground floor. My wife, I, and the children occupy the bedroom. The servant had another. I got the key. I don't know who handed it to me. I went up to the bedroom, and found the door locked. My lodgers have nothing to do with my apartment. When I got in I found my boy, Alfred James, lying on the floor; he had fallen out of bed. I picked him up and placed him in bed with his brother, in the bed from which he had fallen.

They had the bed together in my room. There was no light in the room, but the lamp outside gave a glimmering light, sufficient to see anyone in the room. I turned round to see the deceased, wondering she had not woke up by the noise. She was in the bed I and my wife occupy. I found her close to the wall, lying on her back, with her clothes thrown off her. The bed was close to the wall.

Her head was near the pillow. I reached over and caught hold of her legs. Her head was about 3 inches from the wall. It did not touch it. The bed was on the mattress, it was narrower, and did not completely cover the mattress. Her head was a little higher than the remainder of her body. The mattress was nearly touching the wall. There was not room for her head to get between. The bed sloped off. There was no crevice in which her head could get fixed. She had her nightgown on. The bed clothes looked as if they'd been kicked off. She was in the habit of kicking off the bed clothes. She was very strong in her limbs and her bodily powers, and able to deal with any complication of the bedclothes over her. I caught hold of her by the leg and pulled her towards me, and said "my poor child is dead;" she was perfectly cold. I could tell by the deadweight that she was dead.

My wife came up, and took her downstairs, from my arm into the sitting room. I followed her; the prisoner came down, and stood very unconcerned, as if nothing had occurred. I sent, and Dr. Williams came. He pronounced her dead. I asked the prisoner when she last saw it alive; she said '10:30, in the middle of the bed;' I said 'I don't believe it;' she made no reply. There was an inquest on 13 April. The bedclothes consisted of a sheet, single blanket, and a Macella counterpane, very light. The child was never subject to fits. It had recovered about six weeks from a slight hooping right cough. Mr. Cottrell, his wife, and one child, and Mrs. Brands were my lodgers. Mr. Cottrell's child was six or seven years old. They occupied the first floor above my room. Mr. Broster, his wife, and three grown-up daughters occupied the second floor. The third floor was occupied by Mr. and Mrs. Grains, and a grown-up daughter. Their occupations were distinct from each other, and my part of the house. Six steps leading up to my bedroom, and were part of the general flight upstairs. Everybody would have to pass by my bedroom. I always desired to have the door locked, my key brought down after the children went to bed.

Cross-examined by Mr. Thomas.

Before Good Friday, the day this happened, the prisoner had been with me three days. Her wages were three shillings a week and food and lodging. When we left home the children were in her sole charge for nine hours. She is as much a woman as my wife. I can't say she was feigning sleep when we went in. She got up at about 830 in the morning. I remember saying before the Coroner, in speaking of how I found the deceased. I cannot say positively not having a light, her actual position; as I raised her, she appeared to be on her back or body on the bed, with a head between that and the wall. It was a full-sized iron bedstead. The mattress touched the wall, the bed did not. There was a space between the bed and the wall, of three or 4 inches, making a slight hollow space. Her head was lying partly on the bed partly on the mattress. The iron part of the bedstead would be uncovered near the wall. Her head was lower than her legs.

The verdict before the coroner was 'accidental death'. I said at the inquest I have not seen any want of feeling on Norman's part towards the deceased or any of the children. I never did see any, and should probably say so now. Dr. Williams said that the child had been dead about two hours and a half. I can't swear I heard the prisoner say she put the children to bed about 730.

Re-examined I caught hold of the child's leg to pull it to me. I could not say, positively, that the head was not touching the wall. It might have been. There was light enough from the street lamp to enable to see the head was as I describe it.

ROSINA BEER. I am the wife of the last witness. The prisoner entered my service on 4 April. A person next door, Rosina Lloyd, recommended her to me. The prisoner said she had been in Mrs. Gardner's service, Stockwell Park Road, 12 months ago, and since then she had been working at Army work. She said Mrs. Gardner had gone to Scotland. I thought it no use applying for a character. I was rather pre-possessed with the prisoner she seemed so very clean and respectable. I had three children, all well. The deceased never had any illness; only a slight hooping cough. I wanted no doctor for that. She at this time had been well six, seven or eight weeks. She was a lively child. On Good Friday, 2 o'clock, she was playing with the kitten. She did not eat dinner. It was salt fish and she gave it to the kitten and fell over the plate but didn't hurt herself. We went out at about 245. I said 'be sure and take charge of the children' and she asked if she might have needlework, and I said 'yes I don't want you to do any work, take care of the children.'

We returned at about 1145 to 1150. We went into the sitting room. The prisoner was there, in front of the fire; she appeared to be dozing. My going into the room probably roused her. I said 'how are the children, Agnes?' She said 'oh, very well ma'am, Jessy was rather cross in the park, and I could not keep her from going to sleep.' I had told her never to let them sleep out of doors, in case of accidents. I said 'perhaps she is not very well' but I knew nothing serious could be the matter with her. She said 'the man has not brought the beer.' I said 'you had better make me some tea, I'm so thirsty.' Whilst she was making tea we heard the second little boy scream out. I said to my husband 'run upstairs, there is one of the children fallen out.' He got the key and went upstairs. She was getting a light when he called out 'my girl is dead' I rushed up and he had her quite dead in his arms. The child was brought down stairs I put her feet in hot water and went for a doctor. The prisoner seemed reluctant to go upstairs with the light. She went up when she heard the child was dead. She passed no remarks whatsoever. She was not agitated she never offered to look at the child afterwards. She said she last saw it alive at 10.30, lying on its left side, the same as when she put it into bed.

Dr Williams showed me marks on the lower part of the child's lower lip, about the width of two or three teeth. The gums were perfectly white, as if bloodless. The child had all its front teeth. There were teeth top and bottom, opposite the mark on the lip. The caster would prevent the bedstead coming close to the wall. She was a big girl. There was not sufficient room for her head to have got between the bed and the wall. Her feet were towards the middle of the bed. A quantity of wet had run down on to the palliasse and then onto the floor. It was not dry by morning. It had come from my child's mouth. It made a pool about 6 inches on the surface of the floor. This was between two and three o'clock the same morning. The child was never subject to fits.

Cross-examined by Mr St Aubyn.

Child was very restless, and wakeful at nights, for its age. It usually kicked the clothes off. I found it at times in all sorts of shapes and positions in the bed. I have known it fall off the bed. I have known it to get off the bed of itself. It could not get onto the bed again, not if it had tumbled off. But prisoner did everything I told her to do when we came home this night, and always did. Right I'm going She was quite indifferent, but did not express any sorrow, and looked on more as if it were in her usual work. All the children usually went to bed at 7 o'clock. The deceased was teething. I never gave her fish to eat before. She ate the egg sauce, and had made a good dinner with that and bread. From pain, I daresay, she would kick about a good deal. The girl took the light up to my husband. There was no light up there, but it was light enough to see in the room. Parsonage Walk runs down by the side, and the lamp there enables us to see. I can't say I showed the wet to the doctor. He went upstairs next morning. I showed it to my husband. The wet was not on the wall. I never knew the child to dribble much. Some of my children have done so. The deceased was on the left-hand side to the wall with her back to the wall. What I saw was too much wet to be accounted dribble.

JOSEPH LEES. I am a demonstrator of anatomy, at St Thomas's Hospital. I made the post-mortem examination of the deceased. I saw her a week after Good Friday. The cause of death was suffocation. It was a well formed child. There were morbid appearances indicative of suffocation. On the inner space of the lower lip with two white marks corresponding in shape and size with the two upper front teeth. They might be caused by the child pressing against some hard substance. The pressure of the child's head on the bed clothes would not account for those marks. The nose would protect the child's mouth, a little. I should think the pressure of the lips against the iron band of the bedstead would cause those marks on the lip. I think they were made during life. I think the pressure against the teeth was continued until shortly before death. I could not say within a minute or two. If the child got its head down upon the bed-clothes, so as to interfere with its breathing, and afterwards it had sufficient strength to raise itself by getting on its back, in my opinion it would revive if it had strength sufficient to draw its head out and to turn on its back. If it had died from suffocation by the head being down, caused by the pillow being found over it, it would have been found in that state. If it had got down between the bed and the wall, its head would remain there, and it would have been found dead in that position. It is not unusual after death to throw up mucus, especially after the head is turned down. It is impossible to say the quantity. It would come from the air passages of the lungs and throat. A very small quantity would have made a stain enough to cover a shilling.

Cross-examined by MR THOMAS.

I remember saying before the Coroner that if the child's head had been in such a hollow as has been described, the marks upon the lips might have been made by the force of the child resting upon the lip. The positions were described by the Coroner. The cause of suffocation must be continued a minute or more. I recognise Dr. Taylor as an authority on medical jurisprudence. I have known cases where portions of food remaining in the larynx produce suffocation; even by a pea remaining in the throat; even the close wrapping of a child's head in a shawl may produce suffocation. I agree with Dr. Taylor that where a child is presumed to be suffocated, owing to the position where he has fallen, evidence of the position of the body, or the site of the body, is necessary before forming any opinion. I recognise Dr. Christison as an authority of eminence on matters of medical jurisprudence. The marks on the deceased's lips must've been produced during life. I agree with him that the appearances of a body, the death of which has been caused by suffocation, are in many cases identical with appearances causing death in other cases.

Re-examined if the pea or food obstructed the passages, I should expect to find them in the throat. The throat and air passages were clear. The fact of the marks on the lips afford very strong presumption suffocation was caused by pressure. A person may have gone across the child's face and so produce suffocation; that would be accident.

Q. You have heard the description in which the child was found; from what you saw the post-mortem and the remarks related by the witnesses, do the circumstances exclude or not the notion of an accident?

A. It is a very grave question; I don't like to answer it. If it was shown that the child had went down this hollow place, I could quite conceivably being suffocated there, and the marks on the lips would be caused by the pressure against the iron bedstead. You will not press me beyond my conscience. I can't say sufficiently that accidental suffocation is excluded. I don't believe the bruises on the lip were caused many hours before death. Piece of the lip was removed and examined microscopically, and the mark was found to be simply due to the blood being excluded, and I take it to be pretty nearly certain that if the pressure had been removed before death, the abnormal appearance of the parts would not have been caused. I examine the body eight days after death.

MR THOMAS Q. I want to know whether the appearances presented by a bruise inflicted shortly before death, would not be identical with a bruise inflicted shortly after death?

A. Yes; this is not a bruise, but the mark. I think that if the pressure had been applied sometimes subsequent to death, the same kind of mark would not have taken place. You would have an indentation without any blood being in the vessels. The surrounding vessels were congested. There was no sign of the redness of the gums showing painful teething. If the child had had strength to extricate itself and lay down on its back, it would have recovered.

JOHN JAMES WILLIAMS. I am a surgeon of 116 Walworth Road. I was sent for to Mr Beer's house, on Good Friday evening, about 12 o'clock. I found the child on its mother's lap, dead. She was bathing its feet with hot water. It had probably been dead an hour, or an hour and a half; it would be difficult to be precise. I examined it carefully. I opened the lips, and observed the impression of the teeth. I asked her if she could account for it and she said she could not. It was somewhat strange to me. I have heard the evidence today. Where the bed was, there was not Room enough to enable a child's head to get between the bed and the wall. It might have been on the edge of the bed, and been suffocated in that way. The mark of the teeth was unusual, and could not be accounted for on the lips. The frame of the bedstead would be here. It was a flock bed not very far above the mattress. The bed was not more than an inch, or an inch and a half, in thickness. I suppose the child died from suffocation. I assumed that it might be found dead in bed. I was not told that it was found lying with its head upwards, and no bed clothes on. I saw nothing at the time to indicate its being accidentally done, except the marks on the lips, that aroused my suspicion. These marks were, in my judgement, caused before death, and were the result of external pressure, unquestionably. I saw the prisoner. She was unconcerned; there was nothing special about her. There was no discolouration of the child's skin. I was present at the post-mortem examination, and concur with Mr Lees.

Cross-examined.

I requested to see the bed. I went upstairs and immediately examined it. The mattress projected beyond the bed three or 4 inches. My attention was not called to any fluid on the floor. I put my hand on the sheet, and found it damp. It was where the child had been sleeping near the edge of the bed. The damp had come from the child's mouth. It did not give me any impression of urine. If the child's head had been lying between the bed and the wall, its mouth might cause this moisture. It is possible, if the child's hand had been pressed against its mouth, the mouth lying upon the hand, for the weight of the head upon the lip to cause the marks I have spoken of. The child's stomach was very much overloaded with food. It is possible that the child lying across the bed, with its mouth against the bed, and its head projecting on the mattress, the chances are suffocation will be increased by its having an overloaded stomach. I think it possible if the lower lip of been sucked in by the child, it might produce the mark. The weight of the child's head lying on its face would have been sufficient to produce suffocation. I have known, recently, cases of children dying from suffocation, without any apparent course.

Re-examined.

I have known two cases of suffocation lately, without apparent cause. They were found in bed. One instance was a child lying in bed, with one leg cocked over the other. There may have been some food in the passage to stop the breath. There were no external appearances. In that case, the child was well at 8.30, and found dead at 11.30.

COURT Q. Looking at the circumstances, the post-mortem, the appearances, and the facts, as disclosed by the evidence, is it or is it not your opinion that the notion of accidental suffocation is excluded?

A. Not absolutely, it is possible for it to have been accidental.

JAMES DODD SWALLOW. I am a surgeon, of 285, Clapham Rise, and 61 Kennington Park. I was at the post-mortem examination. I am of opinion that the cause of death was suffocation. I agree with Dr. Lees that the child could have suffocated from the head being downwards, and there being pressure on the back of the head so as to keep the lips and nostrils against the close, it would have died in that position. I am of opinion that if it had sufficient strength to rescue itself from the obstruction it would revive. I've heard the evidence of Mr. Beer, and if he is right in the description he gives of finding the child on its back, I should say it would be impossible to be an accidental suffocation. I rely on it having nothing over its mouth. There was nothing in the throat or air vessels to cause an obstruction. The marks on the inside of the lower lips were caused by pressure against the upper teeth. It could hardly be understood that a healthy child, if lying on its face, with no pressure on the back of its head, would continue in that posture and die like that, without nature making an effort to extricate itself from the posture. To cause these marks inside the lips, the pressure must've been continued up to, and probably beyond, the period of death.

Cross-examined.

It is impossible to tell within one or two hours the time the pressure would have continued on the lips. A bruise or mark made after death is almost identical with one made during life, but this was not a bruise, this was an impression. I saw it eight days after death. A pea, and, such slight causes would produce suffocation or wrapping in a shawl. I have known cases of people lying on their faces being suffocated, in one case, the child was weakly and delicate, through being wrapped in a shawl. I have known children to die without apparent external cause. A child might be perfectly healthy at the time of death, but suffering from catarrh or cold. A child suffering from catarrh, the throat being filled with mucus and having an overloaded stomach, the chances of suffocation would be increased. A child does not secrete mucus profusely after recovering from hooping cough. It is of the first importance to come to a correct judgement as to whether the suffocation was accidental or not, that the actual position of the child at the time of death should be considered. The appearances of the body, the death of which has been caused by suffocation, in many cases are not identical with death from other causes. I think the morbid appearances peculiar to death by suffocation are different to other post-mortem causes. I recognised Dr. Christison as an authority.

Verdict NOT GUILTY.

The verbatim notes of evidence at the trial conclude abruptly with the verdict. Since Dr Christison never gave evidence, it is clear that, at the close of the prosecution, either Mr Thomas made a submission that there was no reasonable case to answer, or the judge himself directed the jury that since accidental death was a distinct possibility, they had no alternative but to return that verdict. It was a total vindication of the coroners' decisions made at the inquest.

The real problem with the case was that by the time the doctor had arrived, he was greeted by the heartrending spectacle of the mother vainly trying to get life in her child by bathing its feet in hot water. The child had been removed from the 'scene of the Crime/ accident' and the state of the art of medicine, coupled with the horrendous rate of infant mortality in mid-Victorian times, had made such deaths all too familiar.

We do get the only description of Agnes Norman that we have in Mrs Beer's recollection of the first interview:

'I was rather pre-possessed with the prisoner she seemed so very clean and respectable.' Incidentally, she was clearly an accomplished liar. The police had no difficulty in finding the Gardners who still lived locally.

Normally, at this stage Norman would have been discharged and free to go. However, she was to face a separate trial on assorted charges relating to Charles Parfitt, which followed on, with the same counsel, immediately after this trial.

What follows is a transcript from the trial for the wounding/ attempted murder of Charles Parfitt, 10 July 1871[3]:

AGNES NORMAN was again indicted for attempting to strangle and suffocate Charles Parfitt, with intent to murder him.

ELIZABETH PARFITT. I am single. I lived in July and August last at 19 Temple Street St George's Road Newington, with my niece, Mrs Brown and her husband. The prisoner came into her service in July. Charles Parfitt was a member of the family. He was in very good health.

About a fortnight after she came, she went out for a holiday. She came back on the following morning, between seven and 8 o'clock. She had leave to stay out. The boys had slept with me that night. I got up about 730, leaving the boy in bed, in good health, asleep. I went down into the shop. About an hour after I heard a noise, a stifled cry. I went upstairs, I found the prisoner in the act of getting off my bed. The boy was in the bed, crying. I asked him what was the matter, the prisoner said that she thought he had been dreaming. He was in a great state of agitation. He heard me put a question to her. He said, 'No I have

not been dreaming, Ellen has been trying to strangle me.'
I called her by that name. I asked her whether it was true,
she said, 'It was not.' He showed me the way and put his
hands to his mouth and throat. He said 'that is the way
in which she tried to do it.' His uncle called him into his
room, and asked him if it was true. That was not in her
presence. She said she did not try to strangle him. The
boy said, 'You did.' He had a sweet in his mouth; I did not
see that. His aunt saw that, and asked him what he had
in his mouth. I was present. He said he had a sweet in his
mouth; Eleanor given it him not to cry. His aunt made
him take it out of his mouth directly. Mr and Mrs Brown
then came upstairs. They called him away into another
room. His mouth was very sore inside the lips. I could not
say what kind of sore it was. For two or three days after,
the glans of his throat was swollen and tender. I heard her
say once she was not fond of children, shortly after this
event. She remained a few days after that.

Cross-examined.

I was living with my niece, as a relation. She was very
delicate, and I assisted her. She engaged the prisoner. I
have never told her father or mother what I have here
today. I never communicated with the police; I told several
people about it. I was examined before the magistrate; I
said, 'I have told somebody of it, Mr Freeman;' I told
Mr Saunders the same day, I believe. They are not here.
As far as I can recollect, I told Mr Saunders the prisoner
tried to strangle Charles Parfitt. I can't say I use the
words strangle before today. I can't swear the boy said
'Ellen has been trying to strangle me.' I believe I told the
magistrate the boys said, 'Ellen has given him a sweet
not to cry.'

This is 12 months ago. I believe I gave the magistrate
the same account as I have given today. I said before him,
'The boy put his hands to his mouth and throat' and said,
'Ellen's been doing so and knelt upon my stomach.' I
thought I had told all today. I took the boy to Mr and
Mrs Brown. They called me. Mr Brown came out on the
landing and took the boy into them. I did not say before
the magistrate, 'Mr and Mrs Brown came and took the
boy away.' I said, 'Mr Brown came onto the landing.' I did
not discover that the boy's neck was swollen till some days
after. I said before the magistrate, 'I looked at his mouth
and found the inside of his lips very sore; his throat was

very much swollen.' I did not send for a doctor, and none
came. I did something for his sore throat. I rubbed it with
Hartshorn and oil. Charles Parfitt slept in the prisoner's
room this night only. The shop is on the ground floor.
The kitchen is on the same floor as the shop. At the top of
the stairs is the bedroom, on the first storey. I was in the
shop. When she first came in that morning she went into
the kitchen first, then to her bedroom, where the boy was
sleeping. There is no doubt I heard this cry.

Re-examined in consequence of hearing that.

I went upstairs at once. I mentioned it to several persons,
I daresay. It made an impression on me at the time.

CHARLES PARFITT. I am 11 years old. I have been
to school. I remember being at Mrs Brown's, 19, Temple
Street, last year, at the end of July, or sometime in August.
The prisoner was there. She had a holiday. I slept that
night with aunt Betsy. I was woken up in the morning by
someone strangling me., with her hand on my throat, and
her finger upon my nose. I tried to make a noise. She gave
me a sweetie. She said, 'Don't cry. Here is a sweet for you.'
My aunt took it away from me. Ellen was on the bed when
I first felt this on my mouth. She was lying on me across
my back. It hurt me inside my lips and throat. When my
aunt came up I said, 'Ellen has been trying to hurt me.'
I did not hear what she said. After some conversation I
went into Mr Brown's room, on the same landing. He
looked at my lips. The next day or so I felt my throat sore.
I was frightened.

Cross-examined.

It is holiday time now. I go to school at Bracknell
near Windsor. I was not very good friends with Ellen. I
did not play with her very much. We did not have many
romps together. I recollect telling the magistrate I had
many romps with Ellen, and used to play with her. I was
asleep when I found Ellen on the bed that morning. I did
not hear her come into the room. The first I knew it was
feeling something on my throat. She said, 'Don't cry, here
is a sweet for you.' I didn't think she was going to hurt me.
I took the sweet from her. I tried to cry out. I didn't cry
out. I made a noise. I could not cry out. The Browns were
in the next room when this happened. I don't know if the
partition is thin. I have heard uncle and aunt talking in the
next room. I don't know in what month it took place it's
so long ago. I don't know which room is furthest, where

the Browns were aware Betsy's was. I don't know when it happened. I recollect going to the magistrates. I don't know who first spoke to me about it. I recollect telling the magistrate I had forgot all about this until a week or two ago. Aunt Betsy never told me nothing. The magistrate was some questions to me. I saw that gentleman (Mr Poland) and in consequence of the questions he put to me, I remembered all about it. He was very kind to me and asked me a lot of questions and answered him yes or no without remembering anything at all about it.

CHARLOTTE BROWN. I am the wife of George Brown, of 19 Temple Street, the prisoner was in my service. She came in July last. I recollect after her holiday her coming back. That morning my husband and I were in bed asleep; I was awoke by hearing the boy before 8 o'clock. He woke me by coming into my room. His aunt Betsy was with him. He was agitated, pale and trembling. He had a sweet in his mouth. My husband was in the room. He had been out of the room onto the landing, and came with the boy and Aunt Betsy. My husband called the prisoner upstairs; she came. I do not know that he said anything to her. I did not hear her say anything to him. I was not out of the room. I looked at the boy's lips almost directly. His aunt said he complained of his lips being very much inflamed inside. I told him to take the sweet out of his mouth, which he said the prisoner had given him not to tell. I did not notice anything wrong about his mouth when he went to bed the night before this. Nor his throat. I notice his throat afterward about the next day; it was very much swollen. Prisoner said she was at the toilet at the time, she said, 'How can you say that Charlie?' He said she was trying to choke him. My husband said nothing to her in my presence.

After some time I asked her what she meant by going into Charlie's room, she said nothing. She said when he spoke of it, 'I was at the toilet doing up my hair when he spoke about it.' I had told her what complaint he made. She said, 'Oh, Charlie, how could you say so?' I don't think Charlie was present then. She ran away on the Thursday following. I gave her notice in the morning, for her insolence. A week's notice. I went over to Mrs Gardner's, where I saw her the same day. She did not expect to see me there. She said she didn't intend going back to me. I didn't know she had run away till then.

Cross-examined.

If Mrs Parfitt said I and Mr Brown fetched the boy, that was incorrect. I had a good written character with her from Mrs Gardner. I kept a few days at my house after this affair. I saw her mother before she left. I told the prisoner in her mother's presence never to trifle with human life. Before the magistrate I said, 'I don't think I did tell her mother now I come to consider, and if I said anything to her at all it was because I dismissed her, because she was saucy.' That is a fact.

Re-examined.

She slept in the same room the boys slept, the night after, with us I believe.

GEORGE BROWN. I live in 19 Temple Street. The prisoner was in my service. When she came home from her holiday that morning, I was awoke by Aunt coming up the stairs. I cried out, 'what's the matter?' I got out of bed, and went to the landing. I met them there bringing the little boy into our room. He was very pale and trembling. He complained to me. I saw his throat. I did not examine it. The prisoner had gone downstairs. I called out, over the banisters, 'Ellen what have you been doing, what you mean by this?' She came up, and I went into my bedroom again. I said the boys said she'd been trying to choke him. She said, 'You naughty boy I have not.' She said she was at the mirror doing up my hair. I think he continued agitated, and trembling, for an hour or two after. He is now generally affected; he will not go to bed, or be left alone. He is especially nervous now when anything of the sort is mentioned.

Cross-examined.

He did not contradict her when she said, 'You naughty boy, I was doing up my hair.' He said nothing. I heard Betsy's feet creaking, as she came upstairs; that awoke me. I don't know the thickness of the partition between my room and this. We can hear people talking. Betsy brought him into my room. That was the first I heard of it. I could not believe, myself, that she could have been guilty of such an act, and I tried to persuade myself it was not so. If it had not been for these other things we have heard of, you would probably not have heard of this case at all.

GUILTY, recommended to mercy by the jury, on account of her youth.

> Judgement respited: If it had not been for these other
> things we have heard of, you would probably not have
> heard of this case at all.

The following month, Norman was brought back for sentencing
and sentenced to ten years.

It would appear that the second case was heard by the same
jury, who were probably somewhat frustrated at not being able to
do anything about the events they had heard that morning. If the
cases had been tried on separate occasions, 'Betsy' would probably
have been acquitted on the second.

As for Sergeant Henry Mullard, like his exemplar Inspector
Whicher, Mullard did not appear to prosper after his famous
case. Police records are extremely sketchy for this period, but
they do record that Sergeant Mullard, still of L Division, resigned
from the force in 1884[1]. He was born in Limerick, Ireland, and
the last record of him in England was the 1891 census where his
occupation was given as railway police constable. This does suggest
an enforced resignation.

PART 2
Louie Calvert

Timeline

1895
Born as Louie Gomersall in Gawthorpe, Yorkshire.

1898 to 1907
Church of England school, Gawthorpe.

1911

April	Census occupation: weaver cloth woollen manufacturer.
13 July	Is charged with theft by Dewsbury magistrates. Bound over and placed on probation.

1912

1 July	Is charged with theft by Dewsbury magistrates. Sentenced to twelve months' borstal by Leeds West Riding quarter sessions.
April – November	Armley Prison, Leeds.
November	Borstal wing, Holloway Prison, London. Transferred to Aylesbury.

1913

13 June	Is discharged on licence.
2 September	Licence is revoked. Stealing landlady's goods and sent back to Aylesbury.
27 November	Discharged a second time.

1914

27 October	Is charged with theft by Dewsbury magistrates. Sentenced to three months.

1915

7 September	Is charged with theft by Dewsbury magistrates. Sentenced to three months.
Late-1915	Probable birth of Annie Gomersall.

1917

9 March   Is charged with theft by Leeds petty sessions. Sentenced to three months.

30 October   Is charged with theft by Bradford petty Sessions. Sentenced to one month.

1920

April   Son 'Kenneth Jackson' is born.

1921

3 January   Is charged with breaking and entering by West Riding quarter sessions. Sentenced to six months' hard labour.

Summer   Moves to Leeds. Starts to live with William Frobisher as 'housekeeper'.

1922

12 July   Body of William Frobisher is discovered in a canal. Louie Calvert gives evidence at the inquest as 'Louisa Jackson'.

1924

Spring   Louie meets Arthur Calvert.
               Burglary by an unknown woman at Hargreaves's shop.

September   Louie marries Arthur Calvert.

16 October   Civil complaint is lodged against Arthur Calvert at Leeds magistrates' courts.

1926

27 January   Hargreaves is murdered in Sheffield.

8 March   Arthur Calvert is told that Louie is going to her sister to have the expected baby.

13 March   Baby Dorothy born to a Miss Ward.

15 March   Louie moves in with Lily Waterhouse.

31 March   Louie 'adopts' baby Dorothy, then returns to Leeds.
               Lily Waterhouse is murdered. Waterhouse is seen to return home at about 7.00 pm by a neighbour. Shortly after that, she hears the sounds of people knocking against furniture. According to another neighbour, Calvert leaves the house at about 8.00 to 8.30 pm, fully dressed, carrying the baby, and with a black handbag and a little satchel.

1 April   Neighbour sees a woman entering the house with a key and a bag under her arm around 5.24 pm.

Another sees her around five minutes later, leaving with the bag and a parcel. She is then seen catching a tram at the bottom of the street. She lies to everyone she meets.

2 April	Louie Calvert is arrested and charged with the murder of Lily Waterhouse.
3 April	Magistrates' court proceedings commence.
6 May	Trial of Louie Calvert.
7 May	She is sentenced to death.
7 June	The Court of Appeal refuses her application.
24 June	9.00 am Louie Calvert is executed.

1. The Exercise Book

I came across the exercise book by chance, buried in a Home Office death file[1]. Just in case there was any doubt as to what it was, it had 'Exercise Book' printed on the front. The cover had the Royal coat of arms and was 'Supplied for use in naval and military schools etc. by His Majesty's Stationery Office'. The woman who had used it had filled in some of the spaces left for personal details:

School: left blank.

Standard: 'V11', presumably the top grade of the Yorkshire village school she had left seventeen years before.

Name: 'Louie Calvert 1768', her prison number in Manchester Strangeways.

Commenced: 12th of June 1926 (it was probably the 14th).

Finished: left blank. She had under a fortnight left to live.

Everything was written in pencil. They do not allow pens or other sharp objects in a condemned cell, for fear that a prisoner might commit suicide before being officially killed. Once a prisoner had been condemned to death, they were confined to the cell – in fact a couple of small rooms – watched over night and day by shifts of at least two wardens of the appropriate sex until the executioner called.

The page inside the cover had four quotations.

The first, 'There is so much good in the worst of us ...' was originally penned by Edward Wallis Hoch, an obscure American Midwestern local journalist who had died the year before.

The second, 'Live on what you have; live if you can on less; do not borrow either for vanity or pleasure; the vanity will end in shame, and the pleasure in regret'. Written in the form of verse, it was a quotation from Boswell's *Life of Johnson*. A prison library book?

The third was a trick verse:

Read see that me and not my got.
Up will I love if me love for
and you love you that love for be
Down and you if you shall you must

When read up and down, you will see, '... that I love you if you love me and if that you shall love me, not my love to you must be forgot', and the final couplet:

Leaves may wither Flowers may die
Friends may forget you but Never will I.

This page was followed by a number of puzzles: graphic mazes and cipher. Perhaps some indication of the way time was passed waiting for a hoped-for reprieve. Apart from three or four visits from her husband, and a final eve-of-execution farewell to her five-year-old son, Kenneth, in the company of her sister-in-law and a friend, she had been kept in isolation[2]. At the end of the book was a two-page petition for mercy. Addressed to, 'the Right Honourable his Majistys [sic] Principal Secretary of State for the home department', she pleaded:

On behalf of my two inocent children are left to the mercy of the world. I know that I deserve to die yet why should I have to bear the brunt of the whole crime on my shoulders and the man who is responsible for this and who did the worst be allowed to go free.

She concludes:

I am being punished hard enough with having to leave my children at a time when they need a mothers love and care most and in their inocense they are praying that their mother may be spared to come home to them again my youngest child thinks that I am in London on a visit to the King and I hope and pray that he may continue to do so I leave myself in God's hand his will be done.

If that had been all the exercise book contained, it would have been of little interest to anyone, except for ghoulish memorabilia collectors. But the main body of the book consisted of a 5,000-word autobiography entitled 'my life story'. Twenty-nine pages of continuous, eccentrically punctuated narrative, without material alterations, give a unique insight into the mind and thoughts of a female serial killer.

It is known that this was entirely Louie Calvert's own idea. The governor wrote to the prison commission on 22 June:

> Dear Fox.
>
> As regards Louie Calvert's 'story of her life' it was her own unaided effort, and she received no help whatsoever from anybody. On or about 14.6.26 the book was handed to her and completed on the 18.6.26. The exercise book was given to her to amuse herself with and she was told that she could write what she liked and that it could not be sent out of the prison. On or about 15.6.26 the prisoner told the matron that she had started writing the history of her life and it came into my hands on 18.6.26 and was forwarded to the Commissioners. The book only passed through my hands and the Matron's.
>
> sincerely yours.
> (signed)

2. The Problem with Louie

It must be admitted that most of the material to construct a true biography of Calvert is lacking. What is known about her is only properly chronicled from late March 1926 to her death in June 1926, the last three months of her life.

The other reliable earlier records are such court records and local paper chronicles as do exist. The new material is almost entirely from there. The quarter sessions' records quoted were part of bundles that had never been examined since they were put in store. The outer covers are so filthy with the grime of the best part of 100 years, that much of the time spent in the Wakefield archives was in hand-washing.

It is also clear that Calvert's own family of siblings had disowned her long before the trial, and were not speaking to the press. The only evidence in official records we have from her family is that of her mother's sister and her favourite aunt, Mrs Reynolds, who did not speak about her background, and her elder sister Edith, the only source of information about Calvert's children[3].

It is significant that no trace of 'Annie Gomersall', using the information given by Edith, has been found. Edith only knew at the time what she and her mother had been told about Annie. The records of the children's home were destroyed.

Over fifty years ago, I was a commercial intelligence executive
with a major British steel company. Ethical industrial spying was
then, as it probably is now, a matter of scrutinizing public records
and trade magazines, followed by putting fragments of information
together like a jigsaw puzzle to produce some sort of semblance of
the competitive picture, but with many pieces missing. Calvert's
life story poses the same problems.

Henning Mankell, the Swedish creator of *Inspector Wallander*,
writing about a fictional character called Anna, who also came to a
bad end and was of the same age as Louie[4], said:

'Compulsive liars are only successful if they weave enough
threads that are true. Then we believe it, then the lie sails by, until
eventually we find that their whole world is built out of lies.'

Calvert was certainly a compulsive liar, but not a successful
one. Perhaps the reason for her lack of success was her failure to
weave enough threads that were true. Yet there were some truthful
threads – most of the time. The initial traumatic brush with the
law, induced by a malicious older sister and resulting in a harsh
sentence, which she blames for her evil life, is fiction, but some of
the basic facts of the offence were true of a later case. There are
some indications that there was an earlier incident that may be
true in part, involving her sister's wage packet. But why would her
sister, who had married in 1908 and was living away from home
in a one-room lodging with her husband, be bringing her wage
packets to her mother?

According to the life story, the most important male in
Calvert's life, apart from her own child Kenneth, was someone
called Jim Jackson. We are told by her that he was a captain in
communications and died in 1920 in India. It turns out that Jim
Jackson was probably, as one might expect, an ordinary sapper in
the Royal Engineers, considerably older than Calvert, and who had
dropped her for a younger woman whom he married in 1922[5]. He
was certainly dead so far as Calvert was concerned.

[Page 1]
Born of humble parents in a country vilage of Gawthorpe
in Yorkshire, I attended the Church of England council
school from the age of 3 till the age of 12 when I passed
my labour examination and left school. I had a very good
schoolmistress and she taught me every thing that was
benificial for me and at home I was taught as a little child
to say my prayers at my Mothers knee. We were a family of
six children 2 sisters and 3 brothers I was the youngest but
one. Ours was a good christian home and father always

used to read prayers and the portion of the Bible morning
and night, we were sent to sunday school and had to go
to church both morning and night. I was quite happy and
contented with my surroundings and Mother never knew
a moments worry from any of us.

Calvert grew up in Gawthorpe where she was based until she was
in her twenties. Gawthorpe is in West Yorkshire on the northern
outskirts of Ossett. For many years, Gawthorpe was considered a
separate hamlet, but in 1866, it was joined with Ossett to become
Ossett-cum-Gawthorpe. The other small towns nearby, Batley,
Dewsbury and Wakefield, feature strongly in her work history.

Like most English villages then, Gawthorpe was self-contained.
There were greengrocers, confectioners, butchers, blacksmiths,
shoemakers, bakers, barbers and ale sellers, all of whom plied their
trade at the end of the nineteenth century[6]. The villagers did not
have much in the way of transport, so local shops competed on
price and quality alone.

The main sources of employment throughout the area were
the coal mines and the woollen mills. Coalmining was a consistent
source of employment for a century, the last coalmine in Gawthorpe
closing in the 1960s. The mills were subject to economic cycles,
the local ones opening and closing to match such fluctuations. If
you were a member of a weaving family, you were more likely to be
kept in employment.

The Church of England school would have been the National
School in Gawthorpe, which Calvert attended from 1898–99 to
1907. According to the 1911 census, Smith was caretaker at the
school.

The Gomersall family.

Calvert's father, Smith Gomersall, was born in 1858, a
third-generation wool weaver. Members of his family had been
self-employed rag merchants, supplying the trade in mungo, a
fibrous, woollen material generated from waste fabric. Mungo
manufacturing was a specialty of the Gawthorpe-Ossett area.

When he was 21, Gomersall married Caroline Dews, a local
girl and daughter of a wool spinner. Their son, George William,
was born in 1881, but Caroline died the following year, leaving
Smith to make arrangements for the care of George. Smith
married Annie Elizabeth Clarke in 1885. Smith and Annie were a
devoutly religious couple. It is noticeable that he is only mentioned
by Calvert this once, and then in a religious context. He became
a deacon of the Zion Congregational Church in Gawthorpe, and

in 1904, he became a trustee of the recently purchased church burial ground. He must have been highly thought of within the congregation, since his fellow trustees were mainly managers and shopkeepers. He bought a burial plot for himself and his family for over £5 – about a fortnight's wages – demonstrating that the family were not poverty stricken.

The mystery about Smith is that at some time between 1906 and the 1911 census, he appears to have changed his Christian denomination, moving from Congregationalist to Methodist. By 1911, he was caretaker to the Church of England school, living in tied accommodation. When he died at the end of 1914, he was not buried in his purchased plot, but in a Methodist graveyard. He died in a coma of arteriosclerosis. The explanation could lie in that, increasing, perhaps permanent, ill-health, had driven him to a sheltered occupation, and the Zion church could not help.

Calvert's mother, Annie, appears in her story as the real head of the family. She was born in 1867, marrying Smith, who was twelve years older, in 1885. It is significant that she is always the one who gives evidence in court and to the police, not Smith, and is always there for Calvert throughout her life. Although she supported the committal to borstal, in the hope that something could be done, she was clearly in touch with Calvert throughout the borstal experience and beyond. Indeed, Calvert states that she looked after her first child from birth until her mother's death four years later.

Calvert had four siblings, not five. The 1911 census, completed by her father, discloses that he had five children, all born alive, and therefore the figure of six in her biography is an uncorrected mistake.

Her half-brother, George William, was fourteen years older than she was, and already working as a coal haulier when she was born. He does not feature in the biography. He married and died in 1940, having lived all his life in Ossett.

Calvert's elder sister, Hilda, was born in 1887. Eight years older than Calvert, she married Willie Day in 1908, when she was 13 and still at school. The 1911 census records that they lived in their own one-room flat in Dewsbury. So far as one can tell from Edith's police statements in 1926, she was still living in Dewsbury. She died in 1933. Clearly a hate figure in Calvert's lexicon. It is probable, due to the resemblances in the photograph of the girls in the Pierrette costumes, that she was part of the group. She is the top, right-hand corner figure.

Edith, born in 1890, seems to have been closest to Calvert before the family troubles with her began. Thanks to her descendants, we know more about Edith than the other siblings. She prospered as a blouse maker and was possibly the highest-earning female member of the family. From the early photographs of her theatrical endeavours with the Methodist Madcaps, it would appear she was, though deeply religious, an independently minded, modern woman who enjoyed life when she was young. Like so many women of her generation, she lost her fiancée in the Great War. She eventually married, in 1925, a local farmer over ten years younger than she was. She was the sibling who stayed at home and looked after her ailing parents.

At some stage, the group family photos in the possession of her descendants were mutilated. Not only was any image of Calvert clearly cut out, so was Hilda's. From Edith's statement in the murder investigation, there was some sort of estrangement from Hilda, that probably began at least as early as Annie's death. Harold, the youngest child, was born in 1898. Little is known about him.

3. Early Crimes

From Calvert's exercise-book biography:

> 'Well, at the age of 12 I started work with my sister next to me at the blouse factory as a finisher …
>
> [Page 2]
> I worked till I was fourteen and then I left to go and learn to be a weaver in the mill with my eldest sister. I was very quick and soon picked it up … we had to weave 22 rugs for 14/- and I thought that we were well paid in those days. I got two pieces of each week and that was 28/- I was so pleased when I could take home. My first wages and my mother used to give me a shilling a week spending money. All went well for the first six months that I worked there and I [page 3] worked hard and never had no fines and was never late for my work … then my elder sister got married and left home and all my troubles began has she did not bother to work hard for herself like she had done for Mother and she thought that she could do as she liked with me. She used to go out in the morning after we arrived at work with another married woman and call for about an hour expecting me to keep her loom going for her. I did it at first but I soon got fed up with her always going out and I left her loom stand with the result that instead of always having two pieces like she used to have she would sometimes only have one then she [page 4]

would go home, I'd tell my mother that I had drawn some of her wages and mother used to thrash me and sent me to bed without my tea Now no one was allowed to draw another persons wage unless they were ill you had a doctors note then the tuner would get it for you. Well, I told my mother this but my sister always found some excuse of another and it got to be a regular thing week after week so I ran away from home and told Mother if she wanted any wages from me she would have them to fetch as I was not coming home any more. I told our manager what I had done and when Mother saw that I did not return home on the friday night with my wages she came down to the mill on Saturday Morning and asked for the tuner who at once took her into the office and showed her the wage book for the past six months and she found out that the wages I had been giving her was quite correct.

The unnamed sister was clearly Edith, whose occupation is described in the 1911 census. If the chronology is correct, then this would have been in 1907.

Hilda married early in 1908, when Calvert was 13. The chronology has gone wrong. The episode of the lazy, lying sister could be a reflection of some sort of family row. It is unlikely that Annie would have had any interest in Hilda's wage packet as a married woman. Certainly, by 1911 Hilda was living with her husband Willie, a coal miner, in Dewsbury.

In the same census, Calvert was living at home. Her occupation was 'Weaver cloth-woollen Manufacturer'. This was three months before she was brought to court for the first time.

On 13 July 1911, the Home Office record shows two charges against her: stealing two pounds, and stealing ten shillings and a gold ring. She was bound over and placed on probation by Dewsbury Borough petty sessions.

No court records of Dewsbury petty sessions have survived, hence the local press reports.

This from the *Ossett Observer*, July 1911:

Louie Gomersal, aged about 20 years, daughter of Smith Gomersall of Pickersgill Street, was charged at Dewsbury Borough Court on Thursday morning, with stealing £2, the property of Emma Nunn, a ward maid at the Dewsbury infirmary, and also 10s and a gold ring, valued at 8s, the property of Margaret Lake, a housemaid at the same institution.

Mrs Nunn stated that she placed her purse, containing £2 in a trial and do not see again until another girl, Aida Dalkin, gave it to her, empty. Miss Lake deposed to placing the 10s and the ring in a drawer on July 10th, in the presence of the prisoner. Inspector Barraclough stated that he arrested prisoner on July 10th. Mr E. Hemingway, the secretary of the infirmary, said she had been employed at the infirmary as a kitchen maid and had been a very good worker, giving every satisfaction, and Mr W.W. Yate, as a member of the board, also spoke, on the girl's behalf, asking the bench, if it was possible, not to inflict upon her the stigma of the prison. The mother of the girl, Ann Elizabeth Gomersal, said that the girl had previously been a weaver and was liable to fits of sullenness. The chairman of the bench (Cr. R. F. Machell) said that the bench decided to take a very lenient view of the case and she would be bound over in the sum of £5, with her mother as surety for another £5, to come up for judgement if called upon within the next six months. She would also be placed under the care of the probation officer Mr R. Parkinson.

This first offence is not mentioned in the autobiography.

Two separate offences involving stealing appreciable sums of money and goods from fellow employees would normally attract imprisonment. The report has her age wrong – she was 15 at the time. She was described as formerly a weaver and, in the 1911 census, which took place four months earlier, that was her stated occupation. It was the family trade and her siblings were all at one time or another connected with the local industry. Was there indeed trouble with her eldest sister, Hilda, in connection with work? Was it hushed up?

Not only had Calvert lost her job as a weaver in three months between census and conviction, but she had been with the infirmary long enough to get a good reference. Calvert must have deeply resented the loss of status involved in becoming a kitchen maid. There is every indication from this court report that the Gomersall family, as a prominent local family, was able to exert sufficient influence that a member of the board of the local hospital was induced to give evidence on Calvert's behalf. Also, note that the mother's evidence of 'fits of sullenness'. By the standards of the time, this would have been seen as an indication of some form of mental illness or deficiency.

On 1 July 1912, Calvert faced two charges: stealing one pound from the mill, and stealing a gold ring and a purse. She was sentenced to twelve months' borstal by Leeds West Riding quarter sessions.

The *Ossett Observer*, May, 1912:

SERIOUS CHARGES AGAINST A GAWTHORPE GIRL

THEFTS FROM FELLOW WEAVERS

At the Batley Borough Court on Wednesday Louie Gomersal, weaver, living with her parents at 32 Pickersgill Street, Gawthorpe, Ossett, was charged with having stolen £1 the property of Patrick Reynolds, fettler, Back Richmond Street, Batley. Inspector Ripley intimated that he intended calling evidence which would justify a remand until Friday. He stated that the girl, who was 17 years old, was engaged by Messrs W.J.R. Fox and Sons Perseverance Mills, on Monday, April 22nd. She commenced work the next day, and gave the name of Edith Annie Broughton of Victoria Road Dewsbury.

On Friday, April 26th a girl named Catherine Reynolds, who worked at the next loom to the accused, received 4s2p, her wages, in a small paper packet after which her father, Patrick Reynolds, who works at the same mill, went to her and gave her a sovereign wrapped in newspaper, with instructions to take the money home after leaving work. The girl placed the money in a packet on the shelf on the loom. Shortly afterwards Reynolds left the room for weft and upon returning found the sovereign, which was in the packet, missing. She complained to the tuner and a search was made, accused assisting, but the sovereign was not to be found.

Next day, all the weavers in the room appeared at work with the exception of Gomersal. On Tuesday the accused was found by the police in Gawthorpe, but she denied ever having worked at Fox's mill, although she was identified by the girl Reynolds. For some time the accused denied having stolen the sovereign, but later admitted her guilt, and said that amongst the articles she had purchased with the money was a pair of eyeglasses at 10 shillings and sixpence. Catherine Reynolds corroborated Mr Ripley's statement in evidence and police Constable Marston spoke to apprehending accused. A remand was granted until Friday.

Yesterday the case was again proceeded with.

Police constable Marston said he arrested prisoner at Ossett and charged her. She replied 'I did steal it. I bought this pair of eyeglasses for 10 shillings and sixpence, and various other small articles with it.'

A further charge was next preferred against the prisoner, of stealing a lady's leather purse, a gold engagement ring, and other articles, value £2, the property of Mary Anne Carter Stainecliffe.

Miss Carter said she worked, along with prisoner, at Messrs. Fenton and Son's mill, Batley Carr, on September 25th last. She placed a purse containing a ring and some money in a handbag, and hung it on her loom, and later it was missing. Prisoner had seen her with the purse earlier in the day, but when asked if she knew anything about the missing articles, said 'I have not seen anybody in the basket.' Witness suspected prisoner, and said she was going to tell the police. Prisoner replied 'don't do that, Mary; wait to we look under the footboard and see.'

Witness later looked at the place and discovered the ring: but it was not in the same spot the previous Saturday. Police constable Marston said that when charged prisoner replied 'yes I stole them: I took them back and put them under the footboard.' Inspector Ripley said he could bring several other cases of a similar nature. When prisoner was arrested, he enquired into her character. The girl's parents were very respectable people, and the mother said her daughter was beyond control, and she would be pleased if she could be placed under the Borstal treatment.

Prisoner was committed to quarter sessions on both charges, and representations will be then made to have a placed under the Borstal treatment.

Calvert's description of the offences that were dealt with at West Yorkshire quarter sessions in July 1912, is totally at odds with the facts proven in court. Her description of what happened follows closely the April 1912 offence against the Reynolds that was the proximate cause of her arrest.

They are described as a single incident, and according to her it was all the fault of Hilda, her elder sister, who tried to get her sacked by constantly putting wrong bobbins in her weft and, by implication, eventually stole money belonging to her partner's father and getting her blamed for it. It is clear from what she says that she has been employed for a while at her sister's mill and her sister was working in the mill at the time of the offence. Hilda couldn't have been working in that mill as Calvert was there under a false name. An unimaginative combination of Christian names:

Edith (her other sister's name), Annie (her mother's name) and a surname that was the name of a nearby West Yorkshire town. According to the evidence, she had commenced work on Monday, 22 April, and it was only four days later that she stole the father's sovereign.

There is no mention in the autobiography of the earlier theft committed, while she was still on probation, against Mary Anne Carter, involving stealing Carter's engagement ring as well as money, and the numerous other offences that Inspector John Marsden uncovered as a result of his instigations.

4. Prison and Borstal

[Page 6]
I said what is the matter Annie she said I have lost some of my father's money well we serched all over without result. When my sister's partner said look in Louie's basket and you will find it. I emptied my weft basket and their I do not know but I was blamed for it and I was arrested and taken to the Town Hall and charged with stealing, I was sent to Armley prison, and remanded for the sessions when I received after waiting trial three months two years Borstall well I was kept at Armley two months after I was tried and then transfered to Holloway Prison in London.

My life in Prison passed on very smoothly and I soon got used to prison discipline and behaved myself well and whilst on remand and I was able to earn a nice sum of money. I arrived in the Borstal in the bigining of November, and their found new rules and regulations for whilst we [page 7] had been in the prison. we were not allowed to talk to one another and it was nothing unusual to hear the officers shout out, Get off your doorstep or stop that talking please, we were allowed to fetch our chairs out and sit talking for half of our every Sunday morning. At the Borstall we work three months in every place and I first started to work in the workroom and we were taught how to make dresses and vairious things. I used to get up in the morning wash and tidy my little cell out and make myself presentable then have breakfast and start work on the workroom till 11 oclock when we would change our clothes for light ones and go and drill for one hour. When we had our dinner after dinner we went for exercise in the in the grounds and back again to work till teatime when on Monday, Wednesday, Friday, we used to go to chapel after tea. Then about twenty of us.

[Page 8]
Girls would go from the chapel to the school and stay for one hour doing school work. I liked the night school better than through the day of course their were two classes in the morning and one in the afternoon and one at night the lowest class being morning. Then I went to work in the laundry and of course I hated washing so I was often in trouble and one day I was that fed up with Officer saying do this and do that I burnt some very delicate work with a red hot iron and of course I was reported well that night, me and three of the girls I was pals with had a real smashup, and we were all taken down to the punishment cells in the Kneebricks and I was put in the strait jacket for striking an Officer for a time given three days bread and water and severn days close confinement and lost some of my remission and not [page 9] allowed to write home for two months and while on punishment. I caught her a severe cold and was taken to hospital with pneumonia and of course that learnt me a lesson I never went into punishment again after I got better. I was put to work on the farm and soon got as brown as a berry...

Calvert was a prisoner in Armley Prison from April to November 1912, on remand between April and July, spending the rest of the time awaiting transfer to Holloway. It was evidently a sort of haven for her, where the rules were easily understood and benignly interpreted, besides she could earn money, which was always important to her.

In 1895, a government report found that young offenders became worse criminals after their release from prison. In 1900, the government set up centres for young offenders called borstals, named after the town of Borstal in Lincolnshire. The Borstal Association was set up in 1902 to improve the treatment and rehabilitation of young offenders.

The 1908 Children's Act, also known as the Children and Young Persons Act, and part of the Children's Charter, was a piece of government legislation passed by the Liberal government, as part of the British Liberal Party's liberal reforms package. It still represents, in many ways, the high-water mark for the movement that regards children and young people as requiring treatment for their anti-social behaviour, rather than punishment for their crimes. It established juvenile courts and attempted to prevent children from learning the 'tricks of the trade' in adult prisons, where children were often sent to serve time if a crime had been committed. It established young offender institutions as a national system, extending it to female prisoners. Provision was made for them for them in Holloway adult female prison and a specialist female young offenders' prison was established in Aylesbury.

The female system at Holloway started badly. An early report by the chairman of the lady visitors as to conditions in Holloway at the end of 1910[1], disclosed that some sort of system had only commenced in February of that year, and this was in chaos.

Essentially, the then prison governor, without proper guidance, had attempted to place those eligible in with the suffragettes and star adult prisoners in a separate wing, but had then changed his mind. Besides, a statistical analysis compiled by the prison chaplain disclosed that of the first forty-five prisoners, twenty-five were prostitutes. There was no segregation, a rather literal meaning for the learning of 'tricks of the trade'. While thirteen were first offenders and sixteen had only one previous conviction, the category to which Calvert belonged, seven had four or more. There was one inmate with no fewer than eleven previous convictions. The nature of offences was varied. Stealing headed the list with seventeen, closely followed by prostitution with thirteen, but three had been sentenced to borstal for indecency or obscene language.

On 1 July 1916, a report on those discharged from the borstal at Aylesbury between January 1910 and 31 March 1916 was compiled for the Home Office[2]. The statistical summary was as follows:

Number discharged, 211.
    A. satisfactory throughout, 94.
    B. conduct doubtful, but not known to have committed
       any fresh offence, 36.
    C. failures: reconvicted: living unsatisfactorily, 81.
    Total 211.

Of this total, fourteen were sent to asylums, considered weak minded, removed early from the institution, or died. An official in the Home Office noted that 64 per cent of the remainder gave, in general terms, a satisfactory result, while 36 per cent were failures.

The report was notable in listing the girls by name, giving a summary for each girl of her subsequent career to 1915.

Among the names on the C list was that of L. Gomersall.

The entry against her name showed her eventual date of discharge as 13 June 1913. Calvert's history after discharge was:

Sent to mill work near Leeds.

Stole landladies [sic] goods.

Second of September 1913 licence revoked and girl taken back to Aylesbury.

27th of November 1913 discharge second time and sent to her own home, Ossett, York, work having been obtained for her.

Working at Mill satisfactorily.

The whole borstal experience must have been a key period for Calvert – she devotes over 10 per cent of her story to it. The laundry incident is not surprising, given her view that laundry work was degrading. But the 'smashup' and its aftermath is the first indication of Calvert's disposition to violence. The straight jacket may have been a punishment, or was it the only way to prevent Calvert from lashing out in her uncontrollable fury?

[Page 9–10]
More Theft when I left the Borstal, I was given along with a good box of clothes a little book with instructions as to what I had to do and did it was this that I had to report at [page 10]

least once a week to the nearest police station all went well for about three weeks then the daring spirit was in me and I robbed my employer of 50£ ran away to Blackpool where I had a good time and enjoyed myself from month on the proceeds when I came back I was sent back to the Borstall to finish my time.

Clearly, according to the Home Office report, the theft, which was surely not £50 (£5,000 in modern values), since that would have resulted in an appearance at quarter sessions and a sentence of several years' imprisonment, was from her landlady, not her employer at the weaving mill.

5. The War Years

On 27 October 1914, Calvert faced one charge: stealing clothing to the value of 3s. She was sentenced to three months by Dewsbury magistrates.

The *Ossett Observer*, October, 1914:

DOMESTIC SERVANT IN TROUBLE
Louie Gomersall (19), domestic servant, of Ossett, appeared in the dock on a charge of Stealing a flannel

petticoat, two embroidered coats and a lace collar, of a total value of three shillings, the property of Mrs Jessica Agnes Lister, wife of John William Lister, of Stanley Terrace, Savile town, by she was formerly employed. Mrs Lister stated that in consequence of a letter she question the girl, who at first denied having taken things, but afterwards admitted having done so, and expressed her regret. Mrs Mary Louise Rayner, of Gawthorpe, spoke to having received a parcel of clothing from the accused, whilst the latter was in the employ of Mrs Lister. She handed the parcel to the police, and the articles were identified by Mrs Lister as her property. Accused pleaded guilty and had nothing to say. The chief Constable reported three previous convictions for stealing against the accused, she was committed to prison for three months.

A vanity/envy theft?

The Home Office report on her, compiled from the information available to them as at March 1915, was not up to date.

[Page11)]
This I managed to get a post as Ward made at the Leeds Gen infirmary and I worked their for four years.

The impression is given that this was stable and continuous employment for virtually the rest of the war.

7 September 1915. One charge: attempted false pretences.
The *Dewsbury Chronicle*, September 1915:

Gawthorpe Young Woman Sent to Prison.
At Dewsbury Borough court on Tuesday, a Gawthorpe young woman, named Louie Gomersall, aged 21, was charged with attempting to obtain 10s by false pretences from the Rev. R.W. Hopkins, Pastor of the Springfield Congregational Church, Dewsbury, on September 4th. Mr Hopkins stated that the defendant went to his house in West Park Street, and produced a letter which purported to have been sent by Mr Arthur Lambert, caretaker of the church. It was to the effect that he (Mr Lambert) had met the defendant on the station platform at Dewsbury, and as she was in trouble and said she had lost her purse he asked Mr Hopkins to advance the girl 10s as he (Mr Lambert) was going away by train. He (Mr Hopkins) took the girl in search of Mr Lambert, who denied all knowledge of the girl or the letter. Arthur Lambert said he didn't know the

defendant at all, and he had never authorised her to take a letter to Mr Hopkins. Detective Sgt Deansfield deposed to apprehending the defendant, who admitted having written the letter, and she gave a false name. Asked if she had anything to say, defendant remarked: seeing this is the first time I've done anything like this, the charge ought to be withdrawn-the chief constable, however, reported that she'd been four times previously convicted. The last time on October 27th, 1914 for stealing coats, etc, when she was sent to prison for three months. Previously she had been convicted of stealing two pounds in cash and a gold ring: and again the stealing a sovereign and a gold ring. At the sessions she was committed for twelve months to the Borstal institution. She was a native of Ossett, but worked at a mill in Batley. Prisoner was sent to prison for three months.

This is the only known early case in which Calvert was involved that was not a straightforward variation of larceny. She made this point in her plea. The background to the case is a strange one. Calvert's father, Smith Gomersall, was, for many years previously, a church-school caretaker in Ossett (Supra). He died on 31 December 1914, some nine months prior to the offence. Calvert was therefore well aware of caretakers and their ways. The crime was typical of Calvert: opportunistic and reckless.

Calvert maintains in her biography that she thought she was married, or went through some form of marriage with a Captain Jim Jackson, who was a communications officer. The internal evidence of the life story is conflicting as to when this 'marriage' took place. One must remember that there were no corrections. Even obvious mistakes, like the number of siblings she had, went unaltered. It makes more sense to the chronology and to the tie-up with the prison record to assume that, when she worked for the hospital, she worked for four months rather than four years. Jackson could surely not have been in France for three years after 1918. If she did work in the hospital for four months, the offence she refers to for which she went to prison at the beginning of the war, took place in October 1914, which meant that she would have come out of prison in December of that year. So, it was the spring of 1915 when she got together with Jackson.

It is gleaned from Edith's statement to the police, that a daughter was born to Calvert in the Leeds Union on 1 January 1917, and was known as Annie Gomersall. It is Calvert's recollection that her daughter was born 'when he had been away in France about four months, and 'I got into trouble again and this time it was a hard sentence for me because I was confined whilst in doing sentence of my little girl.'

So, which offence had she referred to?

She was not in prison in January 1917. The two offences that took place in 1917 were in March and October of that year. She was, however, in prison at the end of 1915. It is likely, therefore, that Jackson had been sent to France in the summer of 1915. So, Annie Gomersall may well have been born towards the end of 1915. It is hard to credit that her husband would accept the daughter as his and go on holiday with her and her mother as she suggests, unless he was around at conception. It is clear that Jackson was a major male relationship of hers. From 1920 to 1924, she maintained that she had been married to a soldier named Jackson, and that her son, Kenneth, was the child of that marriage.

The communications section of the army was part of the Royal Engineers until 1922, when they were separated out to become the Royal Corps of Signals. The local headquarters of the communications section of the Royal Engineers was in Leeds.

Could there have been any truth in this part of the autobiography?

There was certainly no James Jackson serving as an officer in the Royal Engineers during the first World War who could possibly fit the description. There is also no-one named Jackson, or indeed any serving member of the British army, who had died of a sickness in India between 1918 and 1922.

There were of course a considerable number of Jim Jacksons serving in the British army during the course of the First World War. It is therefore likely that she had a liaison with a James Jackson, whom she must have met locally in West Yorkshire, and who had something to do with the Royal Engineers. There is only one entry in the national roll of the Great War that falls within these parameters:

JACKSON, JE, Sapper RE
He volunteered in September 1914, and immediately afterwards proceeded to the Western front. There he took part in many important engagements, including the Battle of Ypres, Loos, the Somme, and Arras, and was wounded on two occasions. He was also present during the retreat in advance of 1918 and after the armistice return to England and in 1920, was still serving in the Army. He holds the 1914 Star and the General Service and Victory medals.
His address (1916) was 15 Orchard Street Hunslet, Leeds.

Further research discloses that a James Edward Jackson features in the register of birth, marriages and deaths, and census returns.

He was born in 1877 and in the 1881 census, he lived at 28 Dresser Street, Hunslet. His father Frederick was a clerk in an iron works. James Edward, according to the 1891 census, was a lithographic apprentice, but by 1901 he had become an ironworks labourer with his father's employer. In 1911, at the age of 34, he was an engineer's labourer and still single. Further research disclosed that he was married in 1923 to a girl born a year after Calvert and twenty years his junior. He died in 1957 at the age of 80.

At the outset of the First World War, it is likely that James Edward Jackson was attached to the Northern Command communications centre in Leeds. As a Hunslet local in his late thirties, it was certainly possible that he formed a liaison with Calvert, who would then have been around 20. There was no marriage, however, and surely Calvert knew that. So why was she receiving a pension/allowance?

On 9 March 1917, at the Leeds petty sessions, she was charged with stealing a costume and sentenced to three months.

On 30 October 1917, at Bradford petty sessions, she was charged with stealing a gold ring and sentenced to one month.

Both cases went unreported – local newspapers had more important news to print at this stage of the war.

6. Theft and Murder: Swallow and Frobisher

> She appears to have kept out of trouble for the next three years. But then …
>
> West Riding quarter sessions records, 3 January 1921.

Indictment:

'That that on 27 November 1920 at Gawthorpe did break and enter/or receive two watches and one guard to the value of 10 guineas belonging to Ruba Swallow. Witnesses, Ruba Swallow, Percy Kitson, Mary Ruth Lambert and John Lambert'.

Ruba Swallow deposed as follows:

> Ruba Swallow, widow, rag sorter of 11 Glenholme Terrace Gawthorpe. I reside alone. I keep the watches under the pillow on my bed. I left home at 6:20 in the morning. Make sure all windows and doors were secure. The door between the coal place and the kitchen is fastened on the kitchen side. Not possible to go into kitchen without forcing it open. Quite sure all secure when I left.

There is a chute into the coal place at the back of the house with an iron grate over it and a piece of oilcloth over the grate.

At 9:30 PM I returned home. I entered by the back door and made down into the cellar kitchen. I made a light. I then saw that the hasp on the coal cellar door was on the hearth rug. I then looked into the coal place and found it had been forced open. I then examined the house and also the bed in the bedroom. I noticed the pillows had been disturbed and the watches were then missing. I then went and saw that the grate had been removed and I left it. I then reported the matter to the police. On the Monday following 29th of November Inspector Lambert showed me the watches and guard and I said they were mine. I should say they were valued at about 10 guineas. I know the prisoner, and have known her for about two years. I am not aware that she has ever been in my house before and had no right to take the objects without my permission.

Percy Kitson deposed as follows:

I am the manager for and son of Daniel Kitson, pawnbrokers, at our Ossett branch. On Monday, 29th November the prisoner came into the shop and offered to pledge the gents silver lever (watch) now produced. I asked who'se it was and she said it was her husband's and he was in the Army. She asked eight shillings for it. I retained the watch communicated with the police and handed it to inspector Lambert.

Mary Ruth Lambert deposed as follows:

I am the wife of Inspector Lambert, who is in charge of the police station at Ossett.

The Inspector asked me to search her (the prisoner) a gold watch and chain were concealed in her left stocking. I then handed the watch over to the Inspector.

(The prisoner here says: – 'the watch was handed over to the Inspector before the witness entered the room.')

John Lambert deposed as follows:

On 27th November I received a report that a robbery had taken place at Gawthorpe. I continued enquiries with reference to it. On Monday, 29th November, I received a message from Mr Kitson, pawnbroker, at 5:15 PM. I went to the shop and received the watch produced from Mr Kitson. I arrested the prisoner as she was leaving the pledge office. I took her to the police station and handed her over to Mrs Lambert for search. I asked her to account for the watch, but she said she had found it in Breach Lane on Saturday night. I told her this watch and other property had been stolen from a house on Saturday night and that I was not satisfied with her story. She repeated her story after Mrs Lambert had searched her. She (Mrs Lambert) handled the watch to me in the presence of the prisoner. I then cautioned her and charged her with Breaking and entering … She replied 'I saw the house in darkness and went down the cellar grate at 7:30 PM. I got the chopper which was hung up in the cellar wall and forced the door. I went straight upstairs. I could not see anyone about. I looked under the pillow and I saw these watches and chain. I took the items and I went out the front door. I stole them to get something to eat.'

Calvert said in answer to the indictment, 'My government allowance of 19 shillings had been cut to 8 shillings and nine pence and I tried to get work. I wanted something for the children to eat.'

She was sentenced to six months' hard labour.

Ruba Swallow

How could Calvert walk into Swallow's house and go straight to the watches under the pillow? On Swallow's testimony, they had known each other for two years. In reality, they had both lived for virtually all Calvert's life within hundreds of yards of each other.

The mystery is really how Swallow, a widow in her fifties, and a rag sorter, came to possess two gold watches. Despite her exotic Christian name, she was born Ruba Jessop in 1865, into an old established Gawthorpe family. Her husband, Fred Swallow, was born a year earlier. He was a carter in the local brewery, unlikely to possess a gold watch. They married in 1892 and had no children.

However, her father was a self-employed clothier, and her parents lived in a row of single-family houses, many of whom had a domestic live-in servant, and which tended to be occupied by engineers – this argues for middle-class prosperity. Certainly, for such a late Victorian family, a gold watch would be an important status symbol to be worn by the head of the family. The 1911 census shows that her mother, Sarah Ann Jessop, by then 85 and a widow, had moved in with the Swallows. She died the following

Daily Mirror

WED JULY 13 1955

1½d

FORWARD WITH THE PEOPLE

No. 16,045 + + + +

'Ban the H-bomb' MP says: I'm going to be a teacher

SIR Richard Acland, the former M.P. is, at 48, taking up a new profession.

In September he becomes a teacher—"a very junior teacher," he says—in a London County Council grammar school.

Sir Richard—twenty-five years in politics—resigned from the Labour Party and stood as an Independent at the General Election on a "ban the H-bomb" platform. He was heavily defeated.

He said yesterday: "I don't want to tell you which school I'm joining in September.

"If I can slip in quietly as plain Mr Acland I shall get a week or two to settle in before anybody comes up to me and says 'Oh, my Dad says you must be the same bloke...

"But if three-quarters of the boys' parents read that I'm going to XYZ school they'll be telling their Willie 'Cor, you're getting an ex-M.P. at your school—re

member to take the mickey out of him ....."

Sir Richard added: "Seriously, I think it might influence my chances of making a success of the job."

He will be dealing with boys of 12 to 14, taking them for maths and science.

"I was always pretty good on those two subjects," said Sir Richard, "and as there's a shortage of teachers I had no difficulty getting the appointment.

"I'm not entirely inexperienced and have often spoken to schools," he said.

"But of course, the Headmaster was always in the hall, so I can't say that I kept the pupils in order...."

THEY WASHED THE SOAP STORE

Sailors helped to quell an outbreak of fire in a N.A.A.F.I. store in H.M.S. Collingwood, the Navy training base at Fareham (Hants) yesterday.

Their task was to spray water over hundreds of cartons of soap which were in danger of catching fire.

CASSANDRA talks to YOU about—

THE WOMAN WHO HANGS THIS MORNING

IT'S a fine day for hay-making. A fine day for fishing. A fine day for lolling in the sunshine. And if you feel that way—and I mourn to say that millions of you do—it's a fine day for a hanging.

If you read this before nine a.m. this morning, the last dreadful and obscene preparations for hanging Ruth Ellis will be moving up to their fierce and sickening climax. The public hangman and his assistant will have been slipped into the prison at about four o'clock yesterday afternoon.

There, from what is grotesquely called "some vantage point" and unobserved by Ruth Ellis, they will have spied upon her when she was at exercise "to form an impression of the physique of the prisoner."

A bag of sand will have been filled to the same weight as the condemned woman and it will have been left hanging overnight to stretch the rope.

+ + +

If you read this at nine o'clock then—short of a miracle—you and I and every man and woman in the land with head to think and heart to feel will, in full responsibility, blot this woman out.

The hands that place the white hood over her head will not be our

hands. But our guilt—and guilt there is in all this abominable business—will belong to us as much as to the wretched executioner paid and trained to do the job in accordance with the savage public will.

If you read this after nine o'clock, the murderess, Ruth Ellis, will have gone.

The one thing that brings stature and dignity to mankind and raises us above the beasts of the field will have been denied her—pity and the hope of ultimate redemption.

The medical officer will go to the pit under the trap door to see that life is extinct. Then, in the barbarous wickedness of this ceremony, rejected by nearly all civilised peoples, the body will be left to hang for one hour.

+ + +

If you read these words of mine at mid-day the grave will have been dug while there are no prisoners around and the Chaplain will read the burial service after he and all of us have come so freshly from disobeying the Sixth Commandment which says thou shalt not kill.

The secrecy of it all shows that if compassion is not in us, then at least we still retain the dregs of shame. The medieval notice of execution will have been posted on the prison gates and the usual squalid handful of louts and rubbernecks, who attend these legalised killings will have had their private obscene delights.

Two Royal Commissions have protested against these horrible events. Every Home Secretary in recent years has testified to the agonies of his task. None has ever claimed that executions prevent murder.

Yet they go on and still Parliament has neither the

resolve nor the conviction, nor the wit nor the decency to put an end to these atrocious affairs.

When I write about capital punishment, as I have often done, I get some praise and usually more abuse. In this case I have been reviled as being "a sucker for a pretty face."

Well, I am a sucker for a pretty face. And I am a sucker for all human faces because I hope I am a sucker for all humanity, good or bad. But I prefer the face not to be lolling because of a judicially broken neck.

Yes, it is one fine day.

Oscar Wilde, when he was in Reading Gaol, spoke with melancholy of "that little tent of blue which prisoners call the sky."

THE TENT OF BLUE SHOULD BE DARK AND SAD AT THE THING WE HAVE DONE THIS DAY.

RUTH ELLIS: CASSANDRA SAYS: "In this case I have been reviled as being 'a sucker for a pretty face.' Well, I am a sucker for all human faces—good or bad. But I prefer them not to be lolling because of a judicially broken neck."

introduction: the Ruth Ellis controversy.

Louie Calvert. (Police Photo)

Louie Calvert. Cover of
the exercise book.

My Life Story.

Born of humble parents in a country village of Gawthorpe in Yorkshire I attended the Church of England Council School from the age of 3 till the age of 12 when I passed my labour examination and left school. I had a very good school mistress and she taught me every thing that was benificial for me and at home I was taught as a little child to say my prayers at my Mothers knee. We were a family of six children 2 sisters and 3 brothers I was the youngest but one. Ours was a good christian home and father always used to read prayers and the portion of the Bible morning and night. we were sent to sunday school and had to go to church both morning and night I was quite happy and contented with my surroundings and Mother never knew a moments worry from any of us. Well at the age of 12 I started work with my sister next to me at the blouse factory as a finisher that meant that I had to trim all the ends of and sew the tapes and buttons make them up into various parcels ready for the various shops I worked there till I was fourteen and then I left to go and learn to be a weaver in the mill with my eldest sister. I was very quick and soon picked it up I learnt in a fortnight and I was so proud when I was put on a loom of my own. It was an Harness loom a great big monster with a lot of cards over the top which got fast now and again if you did not watch it and my first piece of work was a carriage rug with 9 differents colours of weft in it and I had five shuttles going all the same time we had to weave 22 rugs for 14/- and thought that we were well paid in those days I got two pieces of each week and that was 28/- I was so pleased when I could take home my first wages and my mother used to give me a shilling a week spending money all went well for the first six months that I worked there and I

Louie Calvert. First page of *My Life Story*.

Louie Calvert. High Street, Gawthorpe, c. 1911, showing the now defunct High Street stores (later Gawthorpe Post Office). To the right of the shop is the Boot and Shoe public house. Immediately to the left of the building housing the shop, is the Gawthorpe Zion Chapel where Calvert's father was a deacon.

Louie Calvert. Annie (Louie's mother) with Edith and Harold (two of her siblings). The photo has been mutilated by cutting out Louie. Probably done by Edith

Louie Calvert. Two of her sisters. Edith with one pom-pom, bottom left, and Hilda, top right.

Louie Calvert. Contemporary photograph of a handcart in Mercy Street. The suggested means of moving the body.

Kate Webster. Contemporary drawing.

Kate Webster. Contemporary drawing of Mrs Thomas, the victim.

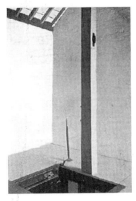

Kate Webster. The purpose-built execution shed in Wandsworth prison, nicknamed the 'Cold Meat Shed'.

Mrs Willis. Two sketch artists employed by the local rival papers (*The Cambrian* and *The Evening Express*) working on different profiles seem to have arrived at the same reasonable approximation of a strong-featured woman with a prominent jaw. However, the reporter for the portrait on the left saw, 'she had big masculine features and a florid face', while the reporter for the portrait on the right saw 'a fine handsome woman'.

Mrs Willis Sunderland wedding certificate, 30 July 1888.

No.	When Married.	Name and Surname.	Age.	Condition.	Rank or Profession.	Residence at the time of Marriage.	Father's Name and Surname.	Rank or Profession of Father.
144	Thirtieth July 1888	Thomas Willis	24 years	Bachelor	Marine Engineer	89 Glebe Street Sunderland	Thomas Willis	Blacksmith
		Emma Dalzell	24 years	Spinster	—	23 Low Row Sunderland	Ernest Dalzell (deceased)	Inn Keeper

1888. Marriage solemnized at *the Register Office* in the *district of Sunderland* in the County of *Durham*

Married in the *Register Office* according to the Rites and Ceremonies of the   by *Certificate before* by me,

This Marriage was solemnized between us, { T. Willis   E. Dalzell } in the Presence of us. { The mark of Michael McIlroy   The mark of Jane McIlroy }   James Christie Deputy Registrar   James Lindsey Sup. Registrar

GMB

1893. Marriage solemnized at the Register Office in the District of Cardiff in the Counties of Cardiff Glamorgan & Monmouth							
No.	When Married	Name and Surname	Age	Condition	Rank or Profession	Residence at the time of Marriage	Father's Name and Surname	Rank or Profession of Father
150	Eighth April 1893	Thomas Robert Willis	32 years	Bachelor	Chief Marine Engineer	Paget Street Cardiff	Thomas Willis (deceased)	Blacksmith
		Emma Dalzell	26 years	Spinster		Paget Street Cardiff	Ernest Cameron Dalzell (deceased)	Publican

Married in the Register Office according to the Rites and Ceremonies of the ____ by Certificate before me.

This Marriage was solemnized between us { Thomas R Willis / Emma Dalzell } in the Presence of us, { Edward Jenkins / Margaret Davies } R J Watkins Registrar / D. W. Evans Deputy Supt Registrar

Mrs Willis Cardiff wedding certificate, 8 April 1893.

Emily Swann, an early 20th-century miscarriage of justice. She was convicted of being complicit in the murder of her husband.

Phineas Gage, a medical example of how brain damage can affect personality.

Agnes Norman The King and Queen tavern, Newington Butts where the inquest on Jessie Jane Beer, was held.

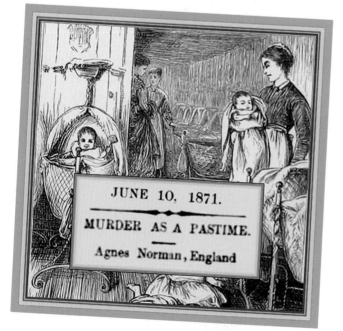

JUNE 10, 1871.

MURDER AS A PASTIME.

Agnes Norman, England

Agnes Norman contemporary cartoon.

Edith Thompson.

year, and any valuables and jewellery she possessed were likely to remain with the Swallows. It is otherwise hard to account for the two gold watches. Could the second gold watch have been a wedding present to Fred Swallow? It is clear that the gold watches must have been the subject of local gossip.

In view of Calvert's subsequent history, Swallow should have considered herself a very lucky lady that she did not return home unexpectedly to meet a 'Cluedo' fate: Calvert with the chopper in the cellar. She lived to the age of 86.

John William Frobisher

[Page 16–17]
I got a post as housekeeper to a widower and I fetch my baby out on the saturday, I was quite comfortable and the man was very good to us both and we always had plenty of good food and clothes to carry on with I was with him 12 months when he happened to go out with some pals that he worked with and he came home quite [page 17] drunk and behaving in a disgusting manner and using foul language in front of the baby and when I told him to stop it he struck me then I started fighting back and struck him a foul blow which caused him to fall down the celler steps and break his neck it was brought in as accidentle death.

John William Frobisher was born in 1873 to a labouring family in Leeds. He was the second son of his father who bore the same name. He had health problems throughout his life. At the age of 16, he was a patient in the Leeds General Infirmary and he was invalided out of the British army in February 1918. He was no stranger to crime himself. The 1901 census found him an inmate in Armley Prison.

He married his wife, Elizabeth, in 1899. She died in the summer of 1919, presumably during the great flu epidemic. Calvert therefore, caught herself a vulnerable lonely widower in 1921.

On 12 July 1922, a policeman wandering along by the canal in Leeds discovered the body of a man in the water. He was found to have a wound on the back of his head and a fractured skull. There was nothing in his pockets and the first inquest was adjourned.

At the resumed inquest, 'Louisa Jackson' appeared. She said she had been the dead man's housekeeper, and identified him as John William Frobisher of Mercy Street, Wellington Lane, Leeds. Neighbours corroborated her story and said she was a familiar figure in Mercy Street in her Salvation Army bonnet and uniform.

The matter had not been referred to the police for investigation and there was no evidence to show how Frobisher got into the canal. An open verdict of 'found drowned' was recorded. During the inquest, the coroner expressed some concern that the man must have been some considerable distance from home to have been found in the canal and with no boots! Louisa explained that she had pawned them for 3s 6d.

The exercise-book explanation would seem to be right, in that Calvert states categorically, whatever gloss she puts on the actual death, that Frobisher died in his home at Mercy Street. He would not have necessarily been wearing boots at the time. The problem is how this tiny woman got the body from Mercy Street to the nearest point of the river, some 200yd, without help and without anyone noticing it.

There is a possible explanation.

A contemporary photograph of Mercy Street in the Leeds archives shows a large, two-wheeled handcart standing outside one of the buildings. In the 1920s, there were, of course, taxis and horse and carts for hire, but poor people relied on handcarts. A handcart being trundled along, even after dark, given Calvert's glib tongue, might escape internal inspection.

There was a last-minute police investigation into the exercise-book story of the widower, which established his identity as John William Frobisher[3]. Two of his sisters were traced, one of whom had attended the inquest and Calvert's trial. She confirmed that Louisa Jackson and Louie Calvert were the same person. The Home Office file disclosed that the exercise-book confession played no part in the decision that 'the law should take its course'.

The remainder of the criminal record is a list of solicitation-related charges.

7. Arty

Arthur Calvert was born in 1878, and died in 1947 at the age of 69.

> [Pages 17]
> I fell out of work through the mill closing down and slack trade and it was a relief when I got on with my present husband, I was at my wits end because I had no money left after I had paid my room [page 18] money ... I had put my child to bed and gone out for a walk to think things over and I met Arthur in a public house and we got talking

about work and one thing or another and I said that I was
fed up so he asked me if I would mind living with him as I
could have a room there if I paid the rent ... it was a poor
home only a table, bed, and two chairs yet we managed
alright and I was glad to have a shelter of any kind over my
head and when trade brightened up again I went back into
the mill were £3-17-0 per week I worked hard and soon
[page 19] got a nice home together I bought Arthur a navy
blue suit as he was not working and I got a few clothes
together for myself and little boy.

I went out more as I used to put my little boy to bed at
night and then go down into the city ... I went to Wembly
when it had been opened the second year and had a
ripping good time I went with a man who had plenty of
money and paid all expences he also took me down to
Soho in London to one or two nightclubs and I quite an
exciting time for a week and he brought me back to Leeds
again of course I would not say who I had been with and
Arthur thought that I had been on my own.

I was not married to him then so I did not care what I
did so long as I enjoyed myself well after I had lived with
him [page 20] just over 15 months his mother came to
see me and told me that she did not like the idea of her
son living tally so he would have to get married I said
its alright you talking like that but where is the money
coming from you know that he his not working and that
I have had to both keep him and provide a home well I
went to make all arrangements about it gave our names in
at the Registers and of course it all came out of my pocket
well our wedding day arrived and I got severe shock when
I arrived at the registors Office for the man asked Arthur
what is age was and he was not sure wether he was 36 or
38 so to make sure as he had lived all his life in the one
house they look through the registar from the date of his
birth well we hunted through all the books for those 2
years and could not find his name as Arthur Harrison, so
his sister who was standing [page 21] for me, is said see
if you can find it in Calvert and the first book we looked
at had his mother's name and his in the Registrar wanted
to put the wedding of and wait another three weeks but I
told him if he did their would be no wedding as I had had
a job to get him to come then so he married us ... well I
went home and my husbands mother came round to wish
me happiness I said you're a grand one didn't like me

living tally did you what about yourself doing the same for forty years and having kids beside.

'Tally' was a form of common-law marriage still in use up north in the early part of the twentieth century for couples who were too poor or too ignorant to get a proper marriage.

[Page 22] ... she for spite said well youve married him and he will never do you any good and before youve been married one month you will be sending him to jail. And by jove it came true has he struck my little boy one night and he fell with his face on the fender and when I came home from my work I knew something had happened for he always came home to meet me at night with his cousin she came byself and said auntie Uncle Arty has been hitting Kenneth and cut his face well when I got home I could hear him crying before I got to the door which was locked so I shouted open this door at once or Ill [page 23] smash it in so when he opened the door I said what have you done to my child you great big Bully he said Ive hitten him for nattering me to go out while someone was at the door my boy was lieing on the couch and his face was just like raw liver I asked him what his dad had done to him and he said Mama he knocked me on the fender.

I took him to the Infirmary and they kept him in and reported the case to the cruelty officer as he had only been home a fornight from haveing been knocked down by a moter car and fractured his scull and they thought that this blow on top of that might affect his brain but however he got over it all right the Dr and Cruelty Officer took the case up and he got 3 months hard labour he told the judge he would swing for us when he came out but however it must have tamed him down a bit for he was glad to get back home again and have a good decent meal the guardian [Page 24] found him a job as night watchman and he stuck it till the job was finished and that lasted four months that was the only time he had ever worked in his life and he has never worked since. So we have lived sometimes on the guardians and when we did not get any money from them I had to go out and get the money fair means if I could and if not by foul.

This story is one of Calvert's 'Romances'.

The gem of truth is that, on 16 October 1925, a civil complaint was made by Calvert in the Leeds Magistrates' Court. It was adjourned. The date of her alleged complaint was 9 September 1925. She applied for a separation order on the grounds of cruelty to herself (she does not mention that in the exercise book) and her child. The only reason for this must have been to get money. At all times, Arty was in work, so why the pretext of having a baby? No convictions registered against Arty under the name Harrison or Calvert in 1925/6.

Calvert says that '... at last I got that fed up with the way we were living and him constantly fighting and drinking that I left home telling him I was going to my sisters and that he can carry on as well as he could.'

8. Death of a Medium

Lilly Waterhouse

Lilly Emily Elsey was born in 1890. The 1911 census discloses that, aged 20, she was the daughter of the house and the lodger was George Waterhouse, salesman. They married in 1913. Her husband died in 1924, leaving her a lonely widow. (see Byrne's statement below and the picture he presents of her.) The attempt in the exercise book to display her as a fellow criminal was particularly despicable. A search of local criminal records discloses no arrests or convictions for soliciting or anything else. The police report about her was merely gossip.

William Alison Byrne, second-hand bookseller, makes a statement to the police on 1 April 1926.

William Alison Byrne was born in Liverpool in 1869 and was therefore 57 at this time. The 1901 and 1911 censuses show that he had been a commercial traveller in ironmongery, so he must have joined the booksellers' trade relatively late in life. He was a family man with three grown-up children.

> I reside at 7 Mares Mount Shepherds Lane, Leeds. I am a second-hand bookseller and have business premises at the shop 19 Park Lane, Leeds.
>
> About the middle of October 1925, a woman came to my shop and said that she had been working for a gentleman in the adjourning purposes and he owed her some money for work which she had done. She said she was ill and had nothing to eat, so I gave her some food. She said her name was Lily Waterhouse, that her husband was dead, that his name was George Waterhouse. I was

sorry for the woman and I continue to give her food each day, when she came to my shop until the end of December 1925 and then I knew that she was getting into arrears with her rent and that she lived in Amberley Road, Leeds. I have never been to her house, although I have had many invitations to go there. I was not satisfied with her habits. I found that she was dirty so I advised and pressed her to go and find work. She said she would do so. I told her I could not keep her in food any longer. From October to this time December 1925, she was at my shop practically the whole day and she ran errands for me.

After this time January 1926, she would call at my shop about two or three times each week. Her visits got less frequent on my directions up to the present time.

About three weeks ago she came to my shop with another young lady and introduce this young lady to me as Louie. Louise said. 'I am separated from my husband.' There was other general conversation and joking. They were in my shop about half an hour and then left my shop to go home. Lily Waterhouse told me that Louie was going to live with her as she had no home and no shelter.

Lily Waterhouse called two or three times a week and on several occasions after Monday, 29 March she has told me that Louie and she were living quite happily together and that when she did call at my shop she said that she had left Louie looking after her house while she was away. The last time that Louie was in my shop would be about 5 PM on Saturday 27th of March 1926. Lily Waterhouse came to my shop one day last week and said 'will you give me half a crown as the board of health want me to have a special bath?' I gave a half a crown out of the 11 shillings which I was saving for her. She had a sulphur bath on account of her having the itch. She was also suffering from some deformity and she wore either shoulder sheets or Irons for this complaint and she showed me a portion of these last Friday, 26 March when she returned from having this particular bath. She said 'They have broken it at the Sulphur Bath.'

At about 10:30 AM on Monday, 29 March 1926. She came to my shop crying bitterly. She said 'oh, I am in great trouble, Mr Byrne, great trouble: I have had a premonition from my husband to look into a bag which I had given to Louie and I looked into this bag and in this bag I found three pawn tickets. One of the tickets is for a gentleman's black suit, another for my best black skirt and the other for a pair of boots.' Louie rose in the bed and saw me looking at these tickets and Louise said. 'They are not yours and you must give them back to me.' I saw that they were made out in the name of Lily Waterhouse. Louie said. 'That does not make any difference: they are mine.' I (Byrne) said 'well, why did you not stick to the tickets when you have them, why have taken the name of the pawnbrokers?' She said. 'What would you do if you were me.' She was crying and very much upset. I said 'you go to the magistrates at about 10 o'clock in the morning at the town Hall and he will give you advice free.' Lily left my shop and went to the Leeds town Hall. She came back to my shop at about 12 noon and said 'I have seen a lady and gentleman at the town Hall, and they said I ought to have kept the pawn tickets when I had found them.' She left my shop almost immediately.

Lily Waterhouse called again my shop at about 4 PM on same day. She had some primroses and she invited me to have some, but I refused. I said 'I suppose the suit that this pawn ticket refers to is your husband suit?' She said 'yes it is.' She then left my shop.

On Tuesday, 30th of March, she came to my shop after dinner and said 'they want to see me at the town Hall at 10 o'clock on Wednesday morning what time had I better leave home.' I said. 'About 9:30.' She showed me two pawn tickets. One was for a pledge for two shillings and sixpence the other I do not know what it related to, but they were both articles pledged in a pawn shop in Amberley Road. I said 'you be very careful that nothing happens.' She said. 'Louise said if I set about you. You are a cripple and it will hurt you.' Lily looked very worried and said 'I will catch the 9.30 car in the morning. 'Lily then left my shop.

She returned again at about four o'clock same day and said 'will you have some primroses?' She had some primroses with her, but I said 'no, I do not want any.' I did not speak to her much she left my shop almost immediately. She came against my shop about midday on Wednesday 31st of March and she said 'I have been to the magistrates at the town Hall, and they have told me to secure the other pawn tickets. They advised me to send Louie to the pictures and get the tickets while she was away. I am very sorry Louie has been so unkind to me

after I'd been such a friend to her.' She then left my shop
– she had only stayed a few minutes.

She returned again just before 5 PM same day. She said
'I'm going home. I want to be home before six o'clock.' I
gave her a cup of tea which he drank. She afterward shook
my hand and said, 'I thank you for the cup of tea.' She
left my shop about 5:10 PM and I have not seen or heard
anything from her since.

On Friday, 2 April, Charles Walter Pass, the detective superintendent
in charge of investigations in Leeds, wrote a report by way of
briefing for the representative appearing on first magistrates court
hearing.

Re-Louie Calvert: Alleged Wilful Murder Of Lily
Waterhouse.

I am instructed by the Chief Constable to place the
following facts before you.

At 11:30 a.m. on Wednesday, 31st March, a woman
named Lily Waterhouse, a widow of 30 Amberley Road,
Leeds, complained at the criminal investigation Dept that
she had missed various articles from the above address
and she suspected a woman lodger whom she knew as
'Louie', as she had found some pawntickets in the house
relating to some of these goods. She also stated to Det.
Sergeant Holland that she was afraid of the woman.

Arrangements were made for Mrs Waterhouse to
attend before the magistrates at 10:30 AM on Thursday,
1st April to apply for process. As she did not attend for
that purpose by 11 AM Det. Sergeant Holland and Det.
Officer Gamester visited the house 30 Amberley Road for
the purpose of interviewing her.

They found the house door locked and the window
shutters closed. They were unable to make anyone hear,
and on making enquiries could not discover any person
who had seen Mrs Waterhouse about during the morning
... The officers opened the window shutters and noticed
that the bed in the room apparently had not been slept
in. Becoming suspicious that all was not well the officers
borrowed a key which fitted the latch lock and entered
the house.

In a small bedroom at the top of the stairs the officers
found Mrs Waterhouse lying on the floor on her right side
apparently dead.

Dr Heyland Smith was sent for immediately and pronounced life extinct.

Information was once sent the criminal investigation Dept and Superintendent Pass and other officers proceeded there to make enquiries.

It has been ascertained that the prisoner, Louie Calvert, is the woman (who) has been lodging with Mrs Waterhouse.

Apparently the deceased first met the prisoner on 15th March last, at about 7 PM in Bond Street, when the latter accosted Mrs Waterhouse, told her she had nowhere to go and asked her if she knew where she could get lodgings. Mrs Waterhouse offered to allow her to live with her and the prisoner accepted the offer. She told Mrs Waterhouse that she was married with three children and separated from her husband ...

On Friday evening, 2nd April prisoner was cautioned and charged with feloniously and of malice aforethought murdering Lily Waterhouse about 8:30 PM on 31st March.

She replied 'it's a lie. I was at home at that time.'

I am instructed by the Chief Constable to ask for a remand until Wednesday, the 7th April to enable the facts to be placed before the Director of Public Prosecutions.

On 3 April 1926, Edith Birkenshaw makes a statement to the police[3]. She is the only member of the Gomersall family to make a statement to the police. Her statement was not used at the trial. She was married to Cornelius the year before the statement. She is the only independent source we have for the existence of an earlier child of Calvert's, Annie.

I am 36 years of age and I am the wife of Cornelius Birkenshaw, farmer, 11 Roundwood Ossett.

Louie Gomersall alias Calvert is 31 years of age and she is my younger sister.

She has two illegitimate children, Annie, now in the Dewsbury union cottage home aged nine years and Kenneth, who, is supposed to be with his mother, aged five years.

Annie was born in the Leeds union on 1 January 1917, and is known as Annie Gomersall and Kenneth was born in a maternity home at Agbrigg Wakefield in April 1920 and is known as Kenneth Jackson.

I have not seen my sister Louie for about two years neither have I had any letters from her but the last time I heard anything about her she was in Leeds.

I have another sister named Hilda Day, who lives in Dewsbury but I do not know anything about her as we do not speak and I do not know her address.

The letter produced is not mine and I do not know anything at all about it.

On 20 March 1926. I went to Gawthorpe Ossett, where I saw my aunt, Mrs Rayner, 7 Glennholme terrace and she informed me that my sister Louie had been to see her and that she was expecting a child at an early date.

My aunt then gave me a letter which she had received from Louie, stating that she had given birth to a daughter sometime in March 1926 but I've since burnt the letter.

I do not know whether she is married or not but I've heard she was living with a man named Calvert somewhere in Leeds.

Deposition of Dr Hoyland Smith taken on 7th April in the Coroners court ... 'Touching the death of Lily Waterhouse, then and there lying dead.'

Dr Hoyland Smith was a source for the chapter on Louie in Berry and Huggett's book[5].

I reside at Hilltop Hall, Bramley, Leeds, and I am police surgeon for the city of Leeds. My medical qualifications are M.R.C.S., L.R.C.P.

I inspected the body of the deceased at 30 Amberley Road, Leeds at one o'clock on the 1st inst, and afterwards at the Marsh Lane mortuary. In a disused bedroom I saw the body of the deceased lying on her back. The left leg was crossed over the right leg. There was a deep pressure mark round the neck, half an inch wide, which had been caused by something having been round the neck, but I did not see anything in the room which could have caused the mark.

There were various bruises on the body. There were two bruises on the head. The hair was matted with blood and on lifting the head I found that the small mattress on which the head was lying was wet with blood, which was oozing from the wound on the back of the head. The other wound was on the top of the head which was only discovered on the post-mortem examination.

There were two pieces of string lying near the feet, but there was nothing on the body at the time. There was also bruising of both wrists the two wrists were together, the right one crossing over the left.

There was a spot of blood on the wall near the head of the body. There was obvious signs of a struggle and possibly the head with the blood on it had touched the wall when falling.

I have made a post-mortem examination along with Dr Taylor, assistant pathologist at the Leeds general infirmary, and the post-mortem report which I now put in and which has been signed for by Dr Taylor of myself is the correct record of my findings.

The cause of death was asphyxia from strangulation. The deceased could not have done this herself. Death was caused by some person other than the deceased herself.

Mr Ould, a solicitor, had by the 1950s become a barrister in the northern circuit, and was a major source of information about Louie for Berry and Huggett.

By Mr Ould (examining for the prisoner):
I cannot give you the exact weight of this woman. She was rather frail and I think she would weigh approximately between seven and eight stones. I did not measure her but I should say that she would be about 5'2" in height.

Great force would be necessary to cause death from strangulation. I did not form any opinion as to whether the woman had been strangled in her sleep or not. She was fully dressed with the exception of her belt and she had no boots on. The belt was lying on the box some distance away. It is a disused bedroom. The bed was downstairs in the living room. It was properly made and had not been used that day. I did not find any instrument in the bedroom which might cause the bruises to the head. It is my opinion that the bruises on the head were caused by a blunt instrument. The bruises on the body might also been caused by a blunt instrument or by contact with the wall or the bed, chair or the floor.

The deceased was suffering from no disease likely to cause death. The only abnormality found was a slight thickening of the valves of the heart and they would not have caused death or accelerated it. There was no evidence of venereal disease. She had skin disease. With regard to the wrists the position of these looked as if they'd been tied. I could not form any opinion as to whether the body had been dragged by the wrists. The strangulation could not have been caused by the string or tape as the pressure mark was much too wide either for string or tape. I do not think it would be a difficult job for a person of small build to strangle the deceased. It would depend in which position they got her: if they got something round her neck at the back of her it would be quite easy to strangle her.

Mr Barnes (for the police):

When I first saw the body the wrists were overlapping. I think they were fastened before rigor mortis started. The entries on the wrists were anti mortem and I think possibly they had been held in that position before the deceased died or fastened by something which had rendered her practically helpless. I should say that a period of quite 2 hours would have elapsed between the fastening and releasing of the hands. I am of opinion, presuming there had been a blow on the head, the instrument by which the wounds had been caused would show no mark as the deceased had very thick hair and I think before the blood got through the hair, the instrument would have been removed. I think it is quite possible that one woman could attack another one and affect strangulation.

Mr Ould (re-examination):

The hands were fastened together before death. It would be very difficult for a person alone to fasten the wrists if the deceased was offering resistance but in view of the wounds on the head, she might have been concussed by the blows on the head and the wrists fastened and strangulation affected after that. I could not say the blows had been effected prior to the fastening of the wrists.

The *News of the World* reported the magistrates' court proceedings in the issue of 4 April 1926:

WOMAN CHARGED WITH MURDER
WIDOW STRANGLED IN COTTAGE
AMAZING STORY
(from our own correspondent.)
Yesterday the opening chapters in one of the most sensational murder cases of modern times was revealed in the Leeds bench. In the dock stood a pale faced woman of slight build, accused of having strangled another, who, from the testimony of the police, had befriended her as the result of a casual acquaintance struck up in the street.

The crime is surrounded by considerable mystery, as deceased had had the reputation of being of eccentric habits and was well-known as a spiritualist, who frequently held seances.

A piece of string had apparently been used for the purpose of causing asphyxiation. There were marks round the unfortunate woman's wrists, indicating that these had in all probability been also tied. Incidentally, yesterday's proceedings disclosed an extraordinary story of an adopted child, which, the police superintendent explained, was taken over by the accused, who told her husband that she was expecting to have a baby. Prisoner, who asserts her innocence in the matter was remanded until Wednesday.

NO SIGNS OF STRUGGLE.

TRAGEDY HIDDEN BY CLOSED SHUTTERS.

'IT IS A LIE. I WAS AT HOME AT THE TIME.'

9. The Trial

The trial took place over two days: 6–7 May 1926. The first day was occupied with the evidence of nineteen witnesses. Arty Calvert was not called.

Mr Justice Wright sums up the case for the jury on the morning of 7 May:

Members of the jury you are here to discharge in this case a duty which is a serious duty and maybe a painful duty. Your duty is, having heard the evidence laid before you, to say yes or no, are you satisfied beyond all reasonable doubt that this unfortunate woman Lily Waterhouse, who was murdered met her death at the hands of the prisoner, Louie Calvert. There is no doubt that Lily Waterhouse was murdered. You can see the photograph, and you have heard the evidence of the police surgeon, and you can see that she could not have committed suicide, that she must've been murdered, and, so far as reasonable inferences would lead one, she must've been murdered by being stunned and then bruised on the body and then at some later stage strangled presumably in a state of unconsciousness and someone also had tied her wrists together and some hours afterwards the fastening of the wrists had been removed.

Now, there is the murder, and no doubt it is a murder. Murder means simply wilful killing of another human being, the technical expression is 'with malice aforethought, express or implied, 'malice aforethought' simply means that it is done intentionally and without lawful excuse; it means the unlawful killing of a living human being with malice aforethought. You have therefore murder but the question remains, who did it? Now the question in this case has been whether the prosecution have brought the case home to the prisoner No one saw the murder, and therefore the evidence must be circumstantial evidence. The evidence of eyewitnesses, people who actually saw the thing done, is called direct evidence. But as very often happens in the case of murder, the evidence must be circumstantial evidence. That is to say, seeing what the circumstances surrounding the case are so as to see whether they link up the accused person with the murder in such a way as to leave no reasonable doubt that that person did the murder and that is called circumstantial evidence. Apparently you are all familiar with that kind of evidence in your ordinary affairs of life and I daresay some of you are familiar with it in the law courts. You had been told in this case more than once that before you can bring in a verdict of guilty. You must be satisfied by the prosecution beyond any possible doubt. The rule is beyond any reasonable doubt. The mere fact that some of you or any of you feel a vague doubt or imaginary doubt or a weak doubt or if you shrink from coming to a decision on evidence which seems to point reasonably with reasonably convincing force to a conclusion, the mere fact that there is some possible doubt is not enough to make you shrink from giving a verdict if you feel in your hearts, in your minds, that there is no reasonable doubt. Now you will bear that in mind of course in considering what verdict you ought to come to here.

Now, how does the matter stands as regards circumstantial evidence? I have no intention now recapitulating the evidence which you have all heard. You have listened to it with very close attention, as I have seen, and with the most conscientious determination to follow it and wait, and I do not want to repeat what I'm sure you all have in mind but to draw your attention to some of the considerations of fact which you may want to bear in mind and consider rather carefully. This is purely a question of fact. You are the judges of fact here. There is really, so far as I know, no matter of law in issue which calls for any specific direction from me. Therefore what I am saying on questions of fact, bind you in no way, though no doubt you would desire me to tell you to some extent how the issues present themselves to my mind, which may help you in coming to what is entirely your own affair, the conclusion of fact. Now what is the class of circumstantial evidence put forward by the Crown, and what are the answers made to it by the defence? Now, there is one fact which does appear to be worthy of your very serious consideration in this case, that is the evidence. I mean one fact. I do not mean 'fact' because it is a matter for you, but there is one class of evidence. One body of evidence which you may consider deserves your very careful consideration. You may decide whether the prisoner did visit that house on the early morning of 1 April, and if she did visit that house and come away with the packages which she is said to have brought with her. From that visit, you may want to consider very seriously. Whether that circumstance, if you find it to be proved, is really consistent with innocence, innocence of the murder. It is not suggested, or I do not know that it is suggested now, that she was entitled to take away the things which, according to the evidence she did take away. Now what is the position about that visit on 1 April? You have first the evidence of Mr David Darley, you saw, but all he says is that somewhere about 5.20 on that morning as the day was breaking saw a woman opening the door of number 30 Amberley road putting a key in the door, opening it with a key, but he could not see her face. She had a bag on her arm like that sort of satchels thing, and so far as he saw she had a long, dark coat and a black hat and he puts the time somewhere about 5.24. He was going out to his work. Evidence as to minutes is very difficult to get in any case. He says about 5.24. He said he heard the door bang.

The next piece of evidence is that of Mrs Dutton, who saw her at she said about 5.30. She said she was getting up to go to work. She looked out of the window and saw a woman coming out of number 30 Amberley Road. She did not know the woman. She said the woman brought out of portmanteau-a suitcase or a portmanteau, such as being described and produced, it looked like something that has been produced-she put it on the pavement. She went back to the house and came back with another parcel, then she went away towards the City Square. According to those times that would give the woman, whoever it was, about 5 min between going in and coming out and going away, anyhow it was not a very long time.

Now, so far, of course, the prisoner is not in any way implicated by that evidence, because neither of these witnesses could recognise her. The next two witnesses speak about the tram, which was at the bottom of the road towards which Mrs Dutton saw the woman which she mentioned going, and that tram passing the bottom of the road had in it Mrs Dunn and a Miss Jackson, two witnesses who have been called, they both tell you – although there is some slight difference in their evidence-that somewhere about a quarter or 10 minutes to 6 the tram stopped at the bottom of the road and a woman got in whom they both recognised as the prisoner. One of them Mrs Dunn, had known the prisoner by sight for some time. The woman was hurrying down to the tram: in fact, the tram had started and it stopped to pick her up, and she was carrying, according to the evidence of Mrs Dunn, a portmanteau – that is the suitcase which you have seen – a basket and a bag, according to the recollection of Mrs Dunn the basket had a white cloth over it. Then Mrs Dunn had some words with the prisoner—I mean passed the time of day and so on, said it was a nice day, and both these witnesses say that the prisoner had a scarf on her head, not a hat and that she was dressed in dark clothes. They both said she had a scarf and not a hat on. Ida Jackson says that what she was carrying was a suitcase, the leather bag, but she also said a parcel wrapped in a white newspaper and a cushion. Their observations as to the exact parcels do not quite agree; they agree to a certain extent. That is a matter which you may consider is not very vital to their evidence. They both agree she was carrying a number of parcels. That takes you up to the point where she's got on the tram, and these two witnesses. If you accept their evidence, but quite precise that it was the prisoner, and although the two first witnesses I referred to couldn't recognise the prisoner, the description or at least the description of the woman who saw the woman come out of the house and the direction in which she went, agree so much as regards time and so on with the evidence of Mrs Dunn and Ida Jackson that you may feel that you must connect the woman who got on the tram with a woman who went into the house and came out of the house, that is to say, connect it with the prisoner. Then there was a boy called, Thomas Reddington, who lives in the same place as the prisoner, who therefore knew her well. He remembers seeing her at 615 in the morning as he was going to his work, and he says she was carrying a portmanteau, a little black bag, a brown basket and a brown parcel – a number of parcels – and that she was carrying them to her house. Then there was a Mrs Morris, a neighbour, who carries the matter a little further, who actually saw the prisoner coming into Railway Place about half past six in the morning carrying a portmanteau, bag and a basket, and according to the evidence of this witness. She said to the prisoner 'you're up early,' the prisoner replied 'Yes, I have been to the station to fetch my luggage home. My sister gave me the things in the basket.' Then Mrs Morris said she saw cups and saucers in the basket, and also boots or shoes sticking out of the bag, and it was these things, according to Mrs Morris, the prisoner told her she got from her sister. It is true she was carrying the things quite openly. You will bear that in mind. Now, in the long discussion or investigation or cross examination, which detective superintendent Pass conducted on 1 April after the prisoner had been arrested she does not appear to have mentioned that early morning visit at all. A lot of things were discussed, and as you have heard from his evidence she did not mention that at all. Now what you have to consider is what is the explanation of that visit and these things being carried away, if of course you accept the evidence of these witnesses that I referred you to. The learned Counsel for the Defence in his very eloquent and able speech for the defence, says that you have to treat it, or you may treat it, is a simple case of theft. Now you may want to take into account how long she was in the house and whether the length of time she was in the house indicated that she had all these things ready prepared the night before to bring away, because that is a matter to be considered very carefully. Of course it is not escaped your attention that the prisoner has not thought fit to give evidence. Well of course she is entitled to take that course. She need not give evidence. She does not want to do it, and learned Council has said there are reasons of health or nerves which induced her or her advisors to come to the decision that she should not give evidence: but when you have difficulties like this visit to the house in the early morning, when you have a difficult incident like that to explain, it certainly would have been-if there is an explanation a very desirable thing that in the case of this sort, the case of this importance, especially to the prisoner, that she should place herself in a position in order to give an explanation. However, I do not want to stress that too much. You still bear the fact in mind that you are left with this incident of the early morning visit from the point of view of the prisoner you have no explanation. She is not bound to give any explanation. She and her counsel were quite entitled to say to you 'now the prosecution has to prove their case beyond any reasonable doubt we are neither going to help or hinder them.' She is quite entitled to take that course. I do not want to emphasise it too much. Here is a very serious fact. If it could be explained you may feel that it ought to have been explained. There it is. You will see there is a good deal to be said as there is in every matter on both sides, and you have to consider in your own minds whether if you accept the evidence of the visit in the morning. That is consistent with what I may call an innocent theft, which I gather is rather what is suggested, what was said at the time the prisoner said all these things had been given to her by her sister, so far as the cups and saucers were concerned, and the other things she told Mrs Morris had been given to her by her sister. As regards the matters as to which she was cross-examined by superintendent Pass or by the other police witness, Sabey, the black-and-white scarf, the suitcase, the sheeting, the cushion, the brown scarf, she said they had been given to her by the dead woman. Then there is a very curious episode about the boots, which you will bear in mind. I suppose the suggestion now is, and you may consider it as a possibility, that if she went in the early morning and found the woman dead, she picked up the boots and any article she could find, and went away with them. You have to consider that as a possibility, but if it does not commend itself to you as a reasonable possibility then of course you may ignore it. You will consider that point. It does not seem possible that this dead woman who was in a state of extreme poverty, in a very unfortunate and sad condition altogether, would have given away all those things in her lifetime, and you may give me think it is quite impossible in her lifetime she would have given away the boots, because, so far as we can see, she had no boots at all left. The prisoner when asked about it, said that the deceased woman had some boots or shoes on and had buttoned boots in pawn, but there is no corroboration of that. In fact no boots, nothing like boots, were found in the house. Now that visit in the morning is certainly a question which you will have to fix some attention, and as regards all these things which were carried away the prisoner gave from time to time different explanations. In the early morning when Mrs Morris saw her carrying the things she told Mrs Morris, who was a neighbour, that she had been to the station to fetch some luggage home. When she was pressed to explain her being out in the morning and bringing things to the house in the morning. She told Superintendent Pass she brought these things from the house in Amberley Road, hidden them in the suspension bridge in the afternoon and then brought them in the morning. Well, this was not true. Of course, because the prisoner is a liar it does not follow that she is guilty of murder. On the other hand it may be you may consider that a number of untruths told to cover up the truth because there is something really serious to conceal. However, that again is a matter to you upon which you must form your own opinion.

Now I have emphasised the visit on 1 April in the morning and the carrying away of these things because you may consider that it is a very vital point in this case, and something which will help you will guide you in coming to a decision. Now as regards the evening before you have to consider the evidence. To what extent you accept it, whether you accept it in all respects or any respect is entirely for you, but you seem the witnesses, and the evidence is that Mrs Waterhouse, the dead woman, came back to her house about seven o'clock. She had been out all the afternoon. The evidence on that is Mrs Popple's. Mrs Popple said she had come back from work somewhere about seven o'clock and she was standing in the street. You will remember she said she lived just about opposite. She lived actually at Oldfield Street, which is not opposite but rather down the street and was passing by on her way home. She was talking to Mrs Clayton and she saw Mrs Waterhouse come down the street, open the door, and go in about seven o'clock. That is the last time that Mrs Waterhouse was seen alive. Very soon after that Mrs Popple, who was still standing in the street, heard

these mysterious noises in the house. She said it seemed
to be coming from the little bedroom. The window was
open. She did not stay long. She listened for two or three
minutes. She said it sounded like people knocking about
or knocking against furniture, and she said it was like
someone hammering a bedstead to try and get it down,
not so hard as if they were trying to get the bedstead to
pieces. It sounded more like people moving about. There
were no cries or moans. Therefore, there were these
mysterious sounds heard by Mrs Popple, and also by Mrs
Clayton. Mrs Clayton was the next door neighbour. She
had seen the prisoner twice in the afternoon with the baby.
She had not seen Mrs Waterhouse since the morning, she
heard sounds coming from the next house, which he put
somewhere between 6.30 and 7 o'clock. She said it seemed
like the boot of a heel tapping on the floor, and it went
on a good many times, sometimes low, then a bit louder.
'Sometimes I could scarcely hear it.' She thought it went
on for about a quarter of an hour, and she went outside,
the noise was going on when she talked to Mrs Popple.
She went indoors again. She thinks about 7:10. Now that
noise aroused her curiosity, because when, according to
her, the prisoner left the house at about 8 PM to 8.30,
fully dressed, carrying the baby, with a black handbag and
that little satchel. She spoke to her and asked her what the
noise was, and the prisoner said that she had been pulling
the bed chair down ready for Mrs Waterhouse to leave on
Saturday. Mrs Waterhouse was leaving the house. Then
she asked her where she had left Mrs Waterhouse, and she
replied that she had left her in bed crying.

Then of course there is the element of the noise, the
fact, according to this evidence, about an hour or hour
and a half after Mrs Waterhouse went into the house
the prisoner left it, and there is the prisoner's statement,
which does not seem to agree with the condition of the
house when it was examined by the police, there is a
statement that she'd been pulling the bed chair down.
She gave another explanation afterwards – that was to the
Superintendent. She said the chair was being put in order
so that if this man, Crabtree, came – this is the man we
heard about – and the house was raided, there would be
another bed to show to the police. That brings the history
up to 8 or 8.30. Then you have the evidence which merely
goes to confirm the fact that the prisoner went home after

leaving the house; she went home, carrying the baby. And she was seen by Florence Hermann and this other girl, Hannah Thompson, in the neighbourhood of the Suspension Bridge somewhere about 20 minutes to 9 or a little later – rather later. Against that a point is made by the Defence that the prisoner's sister-in-law Mrs McDermott, the widow that was called said that she was with the baby on that evening about 7:55 or eight o'clock. That evidence as to time disagrees with the other 3 witnesses who have spoken as to the time. You can decide about that. Then this witness goes on to say that the prisoner when she saw her had a handbag and a market bag with her, and she had a talk with her. Mrs McDermott said to her 'They say you have been in Leeds this last three weeks.' The prisoner said 'no, I have come straight from Dewsbury. My sister gave me 10 shillings to come home.' She was carrying the baby and the market bag and the handbag, and of course she had told other people she had come from Dewsbury and she had not been staying in Leeds. And she told a story to Mrs Clayton, which of course was, as you know, not consistent with the truth. How far you can draw any inference from these particular lies is a matter I can leave entirely to you because they do not seem of so vital importance. On the one hand it is said behalf of the Defence that she was pretending to have got a child and she said she had actually been in Dewsbury, and that this story was merely told to conceal the fact that the child she was producing as the child of her husband was not.

That is the bulk of the evidence. The real evidence that you have to deal with on this occasion, and the central point is undoubtedly will be, you may think – it is a matter for you to consider – you may treat these factors essential facts-first: Mrs Waterhouse went to the house about seven o'clock; about that time there was this mysterious noise; about eight o'clock or thereabouts the prisoner leaves with the baby, the handbag and the satchel and goes home. Then there is the visit the following morning. There is the fact of various things, having been taken from the house, carried away in that way. You will consider whether it may be that they had been prepared the night before and simply had to be called for in the morning. That perhaps depends on your view about the length of time between the observations of the first two witnesses who saw the woman go in and the woman go out. Then bearing all these things in mind you've got consider, of course, the doctors evidence as to the nature and cause of the death. The doctor said that when he inspected the body at one o'clock Rigor Mortis was well advanced. He said that it is very difficult to form any estimate how long, when you see a body, had elapsed since the death. He thought that, and it is most important for your consideration. You have to decide according to the best of your conscience and your judgement whether the circumstantial evidence which you have heard points with sufficient clearness to enable you to say that you are satisfied beyond all reasonable doubt that it was the prisoner who did this matter. If you are so satisfied, you will say so. You are here to discharge that duty of administering justice, but you're not considering any way, you are not to look beyond the verdict you give. You are not concerned with what may happen afterwards. If you're satisfied in the sense I have explained to you, and which Counsel has explained to you, taking into account all the evidence and the way the case was preceded, then you will save the prisoner is guilty, but you must be satisfied beyond all reasonable doubt. If you are not satisfied, then your verdict will be one of not guilty.

Following on from the summing up, the official stenographer notes the end of the trial:

THE CLERK OF ASSIZE: Members of the jury, will you please consider your verdict.
(The jury retired at one o'clock.)
(The court adjourns for lunch from 1.30 to 2.15).
(The jury returned into court at 2.15)
MR JUSTICE WRIGHT: I regret very much, members of the jury, if I've kept you waiting, but the court was adjourned owing to a misunderstanding.
THE CLERK OF ASSIZE: Members of the jury are you agreed upon your verdict?
THE FOREMAN OF THE JURY: yes.
THE CLERK OF ASSIZE: look upon the prisoner. How say you, do you find Louie Calvert guilty or not guilty of murder?
THE FOREMAN OF THE JURY: guilty, my Lord.
THE CLERK OF ASSIZE: you find her guilty, and that is the verdict of you all.
THE FOREMAN OF THE JURY: yes.

THE CLERK OF ASSIZE: Louie Calvert, you stand convicted by the verdict of the jury of a charge of wilful murder. What have you of yourself to say why the court should not give judgement of death, according to law.

SENTENCE OF DEATH.

MR JUSTICE WRIGHT: Louie Calvert, the jury, after very careful hearing, have found you guilty of the murder of Lily Waterhouse. For that crime there is only one penalty known to the English law and it and it falls to me to pronounce the sentence of the court.

The sentence of the court upon you is there to be taken from this place to a lawful prison and thence to a place of execution, and that you be there hanged by the neck until you are dead, and that your body be afterwards buried within the precincts of the prison in which you shall have been confined before your execution, and may the Lord have mercy upon your soul.

THE CHAPLAIN: Amen.

THE CLERK OF ASSIZE: Louie Calvert, have you anything to urge to stay execution of this your sentence?

THE PRISONER. Yes. I am pregnant.

It is clear from what happened next that the court was forewarned of this issue. It was ancient common law that women convicted of capital crimes were permitted to plead that they were quick with child, and to have this claim tested by a group of six women. If the woman was found to be quick with child, then she was reprieved until the next hanging time. Criminal juries of matrons were customarily drawn from the women observing the proceedings.

As medicine improved, the practice was increasingly regarded as obsolescent and rarely used even in the previous century. The author of a leading article notes that a jury of matrons was employed at least once in the twentieth century, by Ada Annie Williams, who was sentenced to death in December 1914 for the murder of her 4-year-old son. She received a reprieve until delivery on account of her pregnancy and, subsequently, had her sentence commuted. The common law was superseded by the Sentence of Death (Expectant Mothers) Act in 1931. Calvert would appear to be the last prisoner to invoke this law.

Jury of matrons:

THE CLERK OF ASSIZE: Mr high Sheriff, let a jury of matrons come.

MR JUSTICE WRIGHT: let all doors be closed and that no one leave the court.

(To the jury: members of the jury, you may now be discharged from further attendance of these assizes.)

THE FOREMAN OF THE JURY: My Lord, may I say one word on behalf of the jury. We wish to thank the High Sheriff of the County of York for the generous manner in which we have been entertained during the several adjournments of the case just considered. We would also like to acknowledge in addition, the kind attentions and the courtesy which we have met at the hands of all persons in whose charge we have been, whether ministers of the court or the people outside who have been catering for us.

THE CLERK OF THE ASSIZE: Will you twelve members now leave the box (the jury left the box).

(A Jury of Matrons was empanelled)

THE JUDGES MARSHALL: You twelve women of this Jury, will you please observe your Forematron's oath.

(To the Forematron) You as Forematron of this Jury shall diligently search and try the prisoner as to whether she be quick with child of a quick child and thereby a verdict give according to your best skill and understanding, so help you God. (The remainder of the jury were duly sworn.)

THE CLERK OF ASSIZE: matrons the jury, your charges now to enquire whether the prisoner, Louie Calvert, be quick with child of a quick child, and give your verdict accordingly.

MR JUSTICE WRIGHT: Matrons of the jury. you may perhaps think it desirable to have the assistance of a medical man. If you take that view a medical practitioner who is inspected the prisoner will be called before you, and you will hearken to his evidence, and when you have heard his evidence you may, if you so desire, retire and personally inspect the prisoner. Would you desire to have the medical witness called?

THE FOREMATRON: yes.

DR HOYLAND SMITH: sworn

MR JUSTICE WRIGHT: you are a qualified medical practitioner

A. Yes.

Q. and a member of the Royal College of surgeons?

A. yes my Lord.

Q. and you are the police surgeon in this city?

A. yes

MR MCFARLANE: have you made an examination of the prisoner?

A. I made an examination about a fortnight ago, when she was in charge of me at the city police station.

Q. did you examine her to make up your mind whether or no she was pregnant?

A. no.

MR JUSTICE WRIGHT: you have not seen her for a fortnight?

A. No.

Q. Then I'm afraid your evidence is of no value. Is there any doctor here who has examined her recently?

MR MCFARLANE: no, my lord.

MR JUSTICE WRIGHT: Then an examination must be made.

(To the witness): you must go and examine the prisoner now, Doctor.

(To the matrons of the jury): would you desire to be present at the examination? Consult amongst yourselves (The jury consulted).

FOREMATRON: Mrs Simpson desires to go.

MR JUSTICE WRIGHT: you will be satisfied with delegating one of your number?

THE FOREMATRON: yes

(Mrs Simpson, Dr Hoyland Smith and the prisoner went below and were absent from 2.45 until 2.55.)

(Dr Hoyland Smith returned to the witness box).

MR PALEY SCOTT: Dr Hoyland Smith, have you made an examination of the prisoner?

A. Yes.

Q. What you find?

A. I find she is not pregnant with a quick child.

MR JUSTICE WRIGHT: Will you explain to the court what that means?

A. any pregnancy had not arrived at the time when the child was quick.

MR PALEY SCOTT: Are you able to say or not whether there is a condition of pregnancy? A. She has signs and symptoms of a very early pregnancy, but I should not be prepared to say that it was a pregnancy. I do swear that she is not pregnant with a quick child.

MR JUSTICE WRIGHT: will you repeat that answer to the jury

A. She has signs and symptoms of early pregnancy. I should not be prepared to say it was a pregnancy, but I do say she is not pregnant with a viable child.

Q. The expression which is used as a quick child?

A She is not pregnant with a quick child.

Q. what does that mean?

A. A child that is quickened, which is usually in the fourth to fifth month – four months and three weeks. She has not arrived at that period.

Q. Do you think that there are signs of an early pregnancy and not a pregnancy which can be called pregnancy of a quick child?

A. That is right.

Q. I suppose a quick child means the foetus has arrived in such a state of development is to live: is that it?

A. yes

MR JUSTICE WRIGHT: (to the jury) members of the jury, you probably understand that better than I do. Do you wish to ask any questions?

THE FOREMATRON: no.

MR CHAPPLE: no questions my Lord.

MR JUSTICE WRIGHT: Matrons of the jury, you heard that evidence. The question you have to try as whether or not the prisoner is quick with the child of a quick child. What that means you've heard the doctor, and you've heard this evidence, and it is for you to decide on that evidence, the answer you are to give to the question which will be put to you by the learned clerk of assize. If any others of you desire a further examination of the prisoner you are entitled to have it, or possibly you may be satisfied with doctors evidence, and with hearing what Mrs Simpson has to say about it. But that is a question for you. Would you desire to make any further examination?

The FOREMATRON. no

THE CLERK OF ASSIZE: will you confer together, Matrons of the Jury, and decide whether this woman Louie Calvert is quick with the child of a quick child and give your verdict accordingly.

(The jury deliberated)

THE CLERK OF ASSIZE: Matrons of the jury, are you agreed upon your verdict?

THE FOREMATRON: yes.

THE CLERK OF ASSIZE: Do you find this prisoner, Louie Calvert, quick with child of a quick child or not?

THE FOREMATRON: no
MR JUSTICE WRIGHT: then there will be no order.
THE CLERK OF ASSIZE: take her away.
(The prisoner was removed)

10. Aftermath

In 1909, the then Chief Constable of Leeds started a unique scrapbook. It was expensively bound and had to be specially commissioned from the printers. The outside cover had the title 'Notorious Criminals', and on the bottom left-hand corner was printed 'Chief Constables Office.' Each double page was devoted to a single criminal. The top third was devoted on the left-hand side to basic statistics: date, place of birth, trade, height, complexion, colour of hair and eyes. On the right was a special place for a typical twin police mugshot, full face and profile. Below that were spaces for the offence and sentence.

From 1909 to 1935, when the scrapbook was discontinued, details of all the notorious criminals of Leeds were entered. In this scrapbook was discovered the only known photograph of Calvert.

In mid-June 1926, the Chief Constable of Leeds, R.L. Matthews, wrote in the scrapbook:

> Name: Louie Calvert.
> Date and place and birth: 1893 Dewsbury.
> Trade: Weaver.
> Height: 4ft. 11 1/2 inches.
> Complexion: dark.
> Hair: Brown.
> Eyes: Brown.
> Offence. Wilful murder.
> Sentence: To be hanged
>
> Calvert was a woman of the low class prostitute type and had two illegitimate children. When in work her conduct was far from satisfactory and she was discharged from her last situation for being 'an unsatisfactory worker, and bad timekeeper. She appears to have commenced a life of crime in 1911, when she was arrested for larceny, and up to the time of the arrest she had numerous convictions for housebreaking, larceny, loitering and importuning, etc.

On 11 May 1926, the Director of Public Prosecutions, writes to the Under-Secretary of State:

Sir
REX V LOUIE CALVERT.

I beg to inform you that the above named, was on the 7th instant sentenced to death at Leeds assize.

Immediately after her sentence the prisoner stated she was pregnant; in consequence a jury of matrons were summoned and a doctor then made an examination of the prisoner and informed the jury that although Mrs Calvert might be in early pregnancy. She was not pregnant with a quick child. The jury then returned a verdict that she was not quick with child and as a result the original sentence stands.

I beg to send for the information of the Secretary of State copies of the Magistrates depositions, statements, police reports, prison medical officer's report and a copy of the doctor's deposition before the coroner. I may add as regards the coroner's depositions that no other evidence was taken, as the inquest was adjourned until after the Assizes.

I have written to the chief Constable of Leeds for the list of previous convictions against Mrs Calvert, who has been in Borstal and has been sentenced about five times for stealing, forced pretences and housebreaking.

The contents of the letter are duly noted and the death file for Louie Calvert is opened on the same day. On 12 May, the Chief Constable of Leeds sends the following letter to the Director of Public Prosecutions:

In reply to your telegram of the 11th instant I beg to inform you that Calvert is 30 years of age and a native of Gawthorpe Ossett, Yorkshire. Both her parents are deceased Calvert appears to have commenced leading a life of crime in 1911, her name then being Gomersall. The list of the convictions are attached hereto.

She has had two illegitimate children, viz: –

Annie, aged 9 years, who is at present an inmate of the Dewsbury union cottage home, and Kenneth, aged six years, who is now living with her husband, Arthur Calvert, at seven Railway Place Hunslet Leeds.

Calvert was married in August 1925 at Leeds and resided with her husband at seven Railway Place Hunslet in this City, until 8th March 1926. She is a known prostitute of a low class.

Since her discharge from prison on or about 3rd June 1922, she has worked at Boyes and Helliwells Rough End Mills, Bramley, Leeds as a Weaver for a few months in 1924, but I am unable to fix the actual dates. She has also worked at Womersley Ltd, Waterloo Mills, Pudsey, as a Weaver from 9 February to 22 May 1925 and in both cases was discharged owing to her being a very unsatisfactory worker and time keeper.

Since her discharge from Womersley's Ltd she has not followed any employment.

Her father, prior to his death, was a mill worker and caretaker, and as far as can be ascertained. He was a person of good character and she, Calvert, was not driven to crime through parental neglect.

The prisoner is of idle and very dirty habits.

I am, Sir,

your obedient servant.

(sd) R.L. Matthews.

Chief Constable

On 13 May, the Director of Public Prosecutions forwarded a copy of the Leeds Chief Constable's report to the Home Secretary.

Was Calvert pregnant?

There is no doubt that Dr Hoyland Smith's opinion that Calvert might be in the early stages of pregnancy caused consternation in the Home Office.

On 17 May, Dr Howard Shannon, the Manchester prison doctor, reported:

Louie Calvert.

Under sentence of death.

I beg to report that acting in accordance with instructions. I have this day in consultation with my deputy medical officer Dr R.W. Walsh made an examination of the above named prisoner. There are no breast changes, no tenderness or swelling nor can any secretion of any sort be squeezed from the breasts. The abdomen is very slightly distended, percussion note is timpanitic all over the abdomen. No tumour of any sort could be felt. Bimanual examination reveals very little. The uterus cannot be palpated owing to some rigidity of the abdominal muscles, rigidity which is, in my opinion intentional. The external os is patulous but there is no discolouration, such as one gets in an early pregnancy. No signs of pregnancy can be to detected on auscultation.

She states that 'she had her last monthly period on first February and that she has recently been sick, i.e. vomited soapy matter in the early morning.' I am informed by the officers who had charge of this woman during the early morning and up to after dinner time that this prisoner has not vomited and has taken her breakfast and enjoyed it.

She was admitted to this prison on 15 April and has had no period since her admission.

If I had to give a definite opinion in this case I should say she is not pregnant, and opinion with which Dr Walsh concurs.

The Frobisher Murder

A garbled report that Calvert had confessed to a Prison wardress about a second killing caused the Home Office to launch an enquiry as to the circumstances of another possible homicide.

On 11 June, the chief Constable of Leeds, writes to the Home Office:

> In reply to your letter of the eighth instant I beg to return here with the original report from Manchester prison, and to inform you that I have no trace of any man having died about 10 years ago in circumstances such as are disclosed in the report.
>
> I have, however, discovered the reports relating to the death of a man named John William Frobisher, who was found drowned in the Leeds Liverpool canal on 12 July 1922, and it is alleged by Sarah Ann Healey, a sister of the deceased, that Louie Calvert pushed him down some steps leading from a bridge, then got the body through a hole in a wooden fence onto the towing path, and afterwards pushed it into the canal.
>
> This allegation seems to have been made quite freely by the woman Healey since Calvert's trial and it is said that that was the first time she had seen Calvert since the inquest of her brother. Healey, however, is a woman of no fixed abode and I have yet been unable to trace her.
>
> After the time of Frobisher's death, Calvert had been living with him for about 10 months and at the adjourned inquest on 21 July 1922. She stated she had not seen him since 10 July.

It was not until 19 July 1922, after the body had been buried, but she came forward. She was shown a photograph of the body but as this was swollen and discoloured. She said she was unable to identify it. She did, however, identify the clothing which had been taken from the body.

At the adjourned inquest. I am informed by the coroner's officer that the coroner pass some very strict remarks to her for not having come to the police earlier to report Frobisher is missing. The verdict was the Frobisher was found drowned but no evidence to show how he had got into the water.

It may be only a very singular coincidence but the fact remains that when the body was recovered, it was without boots; and when the body of Mrs Waterhouse was found, in respect of which Calvert now lies sentenced to death, that also was without boots, and the dead woman's boots were found in Calvert's possession.

As result of other enquiries made it is found that a pair of boots were pledged for four shillings and sixpence on 10 July 1922 with John Edward Nicholson by a woman giving the name of Elizabeth Jackson, 18, Mercy Street, Leeds; Jackson being the name by which Calvert was then known, and 18 Mercy Street being the address at which she had lived with Frobisher. The pawnbroker is unable to say whether the boots pledged were a man or a woman's boots.

So far as I been able to ascertain, this is the only man with whom Calvert has lived who is not still alive.

Yours faithfully,

Home Office minutes headed 'Leeds chief Constable report result of enquiries made...', summarize the Chief Constable's report and comments:

We have only a scrappy report of what Calvert said. It may be that she said 'Canal stairs.' Not 'Cellar' and the woman may be hazy in recollection as two years have passed.

I do not think that she should be further questioned on the subject and her case should be decided without reference to this.

On 19 June, the principal private secretary, writes an appraisal of Calvert's autobiography:

The prisoners 'life story' is dated 14th of June 1926. On page 1 and at the end of her book is a draft or copy of the petition which she has sent up dated 15th of June.

On page 25 of her 'life story.' She says that Mrs Waterhouse, on the Sunday before she was murdered, brought home the next soldier from Beckett Park hospital, who stayed with them for two or three days until Wednesday, 31st of March, the day on which Mrs Waterhouse was murdered. The prisoner says that the three of them had been out having drinks and that the man, whose name was Crabtree, and apparently a Canadian, had brought home several bottles of beer and stouts. The prisoner says the prior to this, there had been quarrels because Mrs Waterhouse wanted the man and the man wanted her (The prisoner). She herself only want to get away, and she was afraid of the police interfering, and she intended to leave that Wednesday. On their return with the drink they got to fighting, the prisoner says that Mrs Waterhouse struck out at Crabtree with her fist and that they both rolled over. The prisoner says. 'I picked up the poker which happened to be the nearest thing to me and my intention was to strike the man and make him leave of hitting her, but instead it struck her on the head through him dodging out of the road that she fell dead at our feet. He went mad, then got hold of her belt, strangled and carried her upstairs. I got out and got home. God knows how I did it, I don't, but I managed to be alright and sane enough when I got there,' etc.

This is of course the first time that the prisoner was told the story. She may have told it to counsel and some of the cross-examination of witnesses was intended to suggest that the woman had been murdered downstairs in the kitchen and had been carried upstairs by a person much stronger than the prisoner to the little bedroom where her body was found.

There are points, however, in the evidence which render her story incredible. Mrs Waterhouse was seen to return to her house about 7 PM by Mrs Popple, it is of course possible that the prisoner and Crabtree had preceded her there and were in the house that time. I've always thought the prisoner had gone to the house in Mrs Waterhouses absence, waited for her to return and attacked her perhaps unaware. (Dr Hoyland Smith evidence which counteract Louie's story is also examined.)

The prisoner says that she struck one blow with the poker and that, by accident, it fell on Mrs Waterhouses head and not on the man; but there were two distinct bruises on the head of the deceased ... Either of these blows would have produced concussion.

It was proved in evidence that the prisoner left the house about an hour later than the noises were heard in the little bedroom ...

The police, when they visited Calvert and railway place on the evening of 1 April, the day after the murder, had found in a handbag a paper with the address of a man called Crabtree 156 Logan Avenue, Winnipeg, Canada, and it appears from the directors paper ... But careful enquiry was made as regards the movements of the miner named Frederick Crabtree of Barnsley. This man was in fact an outpatient that Beckett's Park hospital, and on Tuesday, 30 March, the day before the murder, he was off work went up to the hospital at Leeds with treatment for a wound which he'd received in the war. He appears to have been able, however, to satisfy the police that he couldn't have been the man who left his address and Mrs Waterhouses house and who is the man to whom the prisoner now refers in her 'life story' that having been present at taking part in the murder of Mrs Waterhouse. According to the witnesses who statements were taken. He had a complete alibi. As regards the relevant times on the evening of Wednesday, the 31st, and as regards the previous Sunday when he is supposed to have made the acquaintance of the deceased woman and prisoner ... It seems probable, therefore, that the man who gave the name of Crabtree to Mrs Waterhouse was another patient at the Beckett Park hospital, and that he had either borrowed Frederick Crabtree's name or that he was of the same name.

The British Crabtree's alibi was supported on an hour-by-hour basis by ten witnesses. Was there a Canadian Crabtree?

The Beckett Park hospital only served First World War veterans. Was it likely that a Canadian was still coming for outpatient treatment to a British veteran's hospital eight years after the war was over? There was a Canadian Crabtree, who joined the Canadian army in the First World War, but he was not a native of Winnipeg. Another Crabtree was born in Leeds and emigrated to Canada. Could this Crabtree have been a relative of Lilly's? The address given in Winnipeg existed then and exists now as some sort of store. The only conclusion that can be safely drawn when taken with the other evidence of the investigation, is that the instigation of Mr Crabtree as the principal perpetrator was one of Calvert's fantasies. In any event, the legal doctrine of joint enterprise would have made her equally guilty and subject to the death penalty.

The assessment concluded:

'I do not believe the prisoner story that a man had been present when she struck the deceased woman with a poker and that he subsequently strangled her and carried her body upstairs'.

On the back of the assessment, in handwriting, is a note dated 19 June:

'To advise on Monday whether any weight should be attached to this belated statement. The point was carefully considered but at any rate the miner Fred Crabtree was absolved. Secretary of State to see'.

Below that, in the Home Secretary's handwriting on 20 June:

'I am not sure that I believe all the life story. I shall be glad if some further enquiry can be made as to whether the woman was helped at all in writing it, if not as a human document it is most interesting. The heart of the matter I do not believe and the law must take its course'.

At a minute to nine on the summer morning of Thursday, 24 June 1926, a small group of men silently formed up outside the condemned cell at the end of the wing in the central area of Manchester's Strangeways Prison. Upon a signal from the governor, Thomas Pierrepoint, Britain's 'No. 1' hangman at the time, entered the cell at precisely 9.00 am, accompanied by two male warders.

The two women warders, who had been looking after the prisoner, told her to stand up. Pierrepoint took her arms and quickly strapped her wrists behind her with a leather strap, before leading the way out of the cell through a second door that had been uncovered by sliding away the wardrobe. The prisoner was led forward into the execution chamber by the two male warders and stopped by Pierrepoint on a chalked 'T' precisely over the divide of the trapdoors. The two warders, standing on boards set across the trap, supported her, one on either side, while William Willis, Pierrepoint's assistant, put leather straps round her ankles and thighs. Pierrepoint withdrew what here would have appeared to be a white pocket handkerchief from his top pocket and deftly placed it over her head. H followed quickly with the leather-covered noose, positioning the eyelet just under the angle of her lower, left jaw, sliding down the claw-cut rubber washer to hold it in place.

His eyes darted from side to side to check that all was ready before he leaned forward, withdrew the safety pin, and pushed the metal lever away from him. The hooded form disappeared through the trap and dangled in the cell below.

Postscript: The Attercliffe Murder[1]

Miss Florence Hargreaves, a draper in her early 50s, was an eccentric hermit who lived over her shop at 697 Attercliffe Road, Sheffield. She had started off as a draper's assistant in that same shop and had been running the business for twenty years. The premises were tiny, essentially a ground-floor shop consisting of one room. Her home was the first floor. The shop was to be described as 'very dirty'. And her stock, 'a modern collection of children's garments, blouses, ribbons cottons and silks' was a mess. The window display was more a second-hand clothing junk shop than a prosperous drapers. It was not prosperous. In the middle of the subsequent police investigation, the council's bailiff arrived at the premises to distain for an unpaid rate He was with some difficulty, persuaded to leave the premises, which had by then become a murder scene.

In the spring of 1925, Miss Hargraves was attacked in her shop by a woman who unsuccessfully tried to obtain credit. The assailant escaped, leaving her hat behind, but was never traced.

On Wednesday, 27 January 1926, soaking children's clothing, having been left outside the shop for four days, gave rise to neighbourhood concern. It was not unusual for Miss Hargraves to leave the shop shut for a day or two, but she had not been seen around. An iron gate was usually fixed in front of the door when Miss Hargraves was away. The police were called. Her elderly father was summoned to the premises from Rotherham to supervise the necessary forced entrance. A locksmith brought in to open the front door. The premises were otherwise secure: the back door was found chained and wedged. Any intruder must have escaped into the street during business hours, locking the shop door after him – or her.

Miss Hargraves was found dead behind the counter of her shop. She had been horribly battered. There were wounds in her skull, fractured ribs and her body was extensively bruised. A stocking was tied tightly round her throat, with one long end lying along her back. It was this that had actually caused her death. The case was never solved.

Two months later, when Lily Waterhouse was discovered in her home, it was a copycat killing, down to the use of a ligature, in Lily's case a belt not a stocking, to cause death after a brutal battering.

Calvert had been known to operate in Yorkshire outside Leeds, having been arrested in Bradford for soliciting. After Calvert's execution, the Sheffield police were contacted by an enterprising member of the national press. He stated that, because of the previous assault incident, they were looking for a woman.

It is probable that Miss Hargraves was Calvert's second victim and, therefore, for Calvert, Lilly Waterhouse was a case of third time unlucky.

Part 3
Kate Webster

Timeline

1847
Born as Catherine Lawler in Killane, Co. Wexford.

1864

December   Is convicted of larceny and sentenced to twelve months in Wexford Jail.

1866

March   Is convicted in Liverpool of theft and sentenced to six months' imprisonment.

1868

February   Under the name of Catherine Layles, is convicted of two robberies, being two of an organized series of lodging-house robberies, of which she is guilty. Is sentenced to twelve months' imprisonment upon the first indictment, and five years' penal servitude upon the second.

1871

April   The census lists Catherine Layless, aged 24, as an inmate of Knaphill female convict prison, Woking, Surrey.

1872

28 January   Is discharged from prison. On discharge, she goes to Mrs Meredith's home for discharged prisoners at Nine Elms Mission, Wandsworth Road, living the rest of her life beside the Thames.

1873

4 September   Discovery of part of first 'Thames Torso'.

1874

June   Discovery of second 'Thames Torso'.

1875

April 12   Is charged with three thefts in Kingston upon Thames. Sentenced to eighteen months' hard labour in Wandsworth Prison.

1877

18 January   Is charged with receiving in Kingston upon Thames sentenced to twelve months' hard labour in Wandsworth Prison.

Time Line in Murder trial, abridged from *Notable British Trials*:

1879

March

2   Mrs Thomas is last seen alive at evening service. On her return home to 2 Mayfield Gardens she is murdered.

3   Kate Webster clears away evidence of crime. T. Deane calls.

4   Kate Webster visits the Porters. Robert Porter helps her to carry box.

5   Box found at Barnes

6   Porter calls with Kate Webster at Brook's (greengrocer and furniture remover). Kate sleeps at the Porters that night.

7   Mrs Porter goes to 2 Mayfield cottages.

8   Kate Webster goes to see Mrs Crease. Henry Porter visits 2 Mayfield cottages.

9   Robert Porter reads about finding of the box. Kate Webster is introduced to Church.

10   The foot is found at Twickenham. Inquest on remains in box commences.

11   Church's first visit to Mayfield Gardens.

12   Kate Webster fetches her boy from Mrs Crease's. John Church and Henry Porter visit 2 Mayfield cottages.

13   Church and Henry Porter again at 2 Mayfield cottages. Church pays Kate Webster £18 on account.

14   Weston visits Mayfield cottages. Church is there with Kate Webster.

15   Church again at two Mayfield cottages.

16   Kate Webster on river with Church and party

17   Church and Porter at two Mayfield cottages superintending packing of furniture.

18	The interrupted removal of furniture from two Mayfield cottages. Kate Webster's flight. Last day of inquest.
19	Kate Webster arrives in Ireland.
21	Church and Porter call at the Menhennicks, 45 Ambler Road, Finsbury Park.
22	William Henry Hughes, brother of Mrs Thomas's executor and solicitor, visits the 'Rising Sun'. Accompanied by John Church and Henry Porter he goes to Richmond police station. Inspector Pearman, Mr Hughes, John Church and Henry Porter go to 2 Mayfield cottages.
23	Inspector Pearman goes to 'Rising Sun.' He learns there the story of Robert Porter and the box.
24	Police search 2 Mayfield cottages. Finding of bones, chopper, et cetera.
25	Tuesday, 25th. Police search 'Rising Sun' and visit Mayfield cottages again. Find Mrs Thomas's diary.
27	Further search in Mayfield cottages and discovery of 'fatty substance' and bloodstains.
28	Arrest of Kate Webster at Killane.
29	Police again search the 'Rising Sun'.
30	Kate Webster's first statement with addition. Arrest of Church.
31	Kate Webster and John Church brought before Richmond magistrates. Proceedings are adjourned.
April	
9	Magisterial proceedings are resumed.
10	Kate Webster's statement incriminating Henry Porter.
May	Proceedings conclude and Kate Webster is committed for trial.
July	
2	Murder trial commences.
8	Trial ends. Webster is condemned to death.
10	First post-conviction statement.
17	Second post-conviction statement.
28	Final confession.
29	Execution of Kate Webster, 9.00 am, Wandsworth Prison.

1. A Death Cell Brawl

The rumpus in the condemned cell of Wandsworth Prison, when Kate Webster had less than thirty-six hours to live, is well documented in the Home Office file[1]. As will be seen, the fundamental problem for the prison authorities was the danger of material being passed to the prisoner on a visit (could be poison or to be used in an escape attempt) and the difficulty of keeping Webster under direct and continuous observation.

Letter to Prison Commissioners from Fitzpatrick O'Brien Solicitor dated 24th of July 1879[1]:

> I had the pleasure of an interview with you yesterday when you were kind enough to give me an order to see the unhappy convict professionally for which I thank you.
>
> At the prisoner's desire and written request I attended at the prison today and regretted to find the ill feelings displayed towards her in this hour of trial in peril by the matron. The person I have known there as Mrs Howison and in addition to this the same feelings were evinced towards myself and the ladies who came to see the unfortunate woman (Webster) for the last time. The woman Howison the warden publicly grossly insulted myself and the two ladies who were present, and being reprimanded by me often? for the insolent and intemperate course she'd adopted the Governor was called in by her to endorse her conduct and without any hesitation on his part he ordered me and the ladies at once out of the prison upon the report of the woman Howison the warder. My unfortunate client who had already suffered at the hands of this person was greatly grieved and rendered unhappy but this seemed only to give some satisfaction to the wardress. I left the prison without taking my further instructions being obliged to caution the Governor as to the course he thought fit to adopt my determination to have the matter brought before the proper quarter.
>
> I was never in my lifetime subjected to such insult to say nothing of my legal right and I think it my duty to write to you direct that I have placed the matter in the hands of my consul for an enquiry and I beg you will acknowledge hereof.

The official version is found in statements made by the matron and governor of the prison to the prison commissioners. Mr Coalville, governor of Wandsworth Prison:

> Between 2 and 3 o'clock P.M. Mr O'Brien, solicitor, attended ... accompanied by his wife son and two daughters. I contacted the prisoner to know whether she

wished to see them and she wished to see Mr and Mrs O'Brien. They were accordingly admitted and the usual precautions taken to prevent anything being passed to the prisoner or too close contact. An officer being present, (as the visit wasn't an official one between lawyer and client). Mr O'Brien's manner towards the prisoner being such as to call for the Attendant Officers interference as per the annexed statement taken down immediately after the event and subsequently requiring the Matron to send for me owing to O'Brien's insulting behaviour towards her and which was joined in by his wife also. On my coming on the scene I found Mr O'Brien and party using most loud and unbecoming language in defiance of all order. I immediately ordered him to leave when he turned his insults on myself.

The wife and daughter who had been subsequently admitted by prisoner's request also joining in. I told them this could not be permitted and to move on to the gate Mr O'Brien continuing to use very insulting language the whole way. Amongst other statements that he supposed I knew my brother Col Colville was turned out of Coldbath [Coldbath Fields, a prison in Clerkenwell for those serving short sentences] repeating 'I suppose you know that I had been brought up from Bodmin by Adml. Hornby and that he, Mr O'Brien, would perhaps turn me out of this too etc.' I made him no reply except that he should be careful not to insult me within my own command. His reply 'what would you do then?' I said I would see you to the gate which I did and immediately proceeded to the Home Office and reported to the Commissioner of the District. Throughout Mr O'Brien's former visits there were grave suspicions that he kept much too close to the prisoner and had facilities by so doing of passing things to her. On this day's visit being an apparent friendly one greater precautions were necessary in the way the family shut out the prisoner from the view of the officer on duty was most suspicious. In making this report I must respectfully request that no more unrestricted visits may be allowed if any visits at all be allowed to Mr O'Brien his manner being such as to set all authority of defiance ...

Statement from Miss Hewison, matron of Wandsworth Prison:

The Matron on the occasion of Mr O'Brien's visit to the prisoner Webster left one of our officers, Miss Edwards, in charge having previously given her instructions to use the utmost vigilance to prevent anything being passed to the prisoner. She also saw Mr O'Brien prior to the interview and informed him of having arranged for the presence of an officer, as the visit was under the usual restrictions. A few minutes after it commenced Miss Edwards sent for the matron as an altercation had arisen in consequence of Mr O'Brien's objection to her sitting so near to the Prisoner. On the matron entering the Rome she found Mr O'Brien holding the prisoner's head with both his hands and whispering closely in her ear. The matron told Miss Edwards to move to a greater distance as she did not consider it absolutely necessary that every word said by Mr O'Brien should be heard by the officer. She also explained to him that on no account was any article to be given to the prisoner without the sanction of the Governor. The matron left the scene.

Shortly afterwards there was a request with which she complied that Miss O'Brien might also be allowed to visit the prisoner. The matron had previously ascertained from the Governor that the arrangement she was making was with his approbation. Very soon Miss Edwards again sent for the Matron and complained of Mr O'Brien's conduct towards the prisoner and also the gross impertinence she had received from the whole party while simply adhering to the Matrons directions. The two ladies were sitting on either side of the prisoner when the Matron entered the Room and Mr O'Brien was consulting with the Sister. The Matron determined to stay in the room with Miss Edwards during the remainder of the interview. In a few minutes Mr O'Brien took a chair directly in front of the prisoner who was by this means completely hidden from view by himself and family. The Matron then interfered, quietly but firmly informing him that this could not be allowed. He once became extremely impertinent told the matron to hold her tongue more than once and the whole party were to continue in their[?] heedless of Miss Edwards as well as of the Matron, that she had requested Miss Edwards to leave the room to avoid further insult and that she had sent for the Governor who in a minute or two arrived and put an end to the interview.

Note on the file by a senior Home Office official:

> Better I think to do nothing. He says he has put the matter into the hands of his counsel. It would be worse than useless to send to such a man the statement of Matron and Governor and his own statement is so vague that it is not worth answering. Inform Prisoner Commission that if any action is taken by Mr O'Brien the Treasury solicitors will be instructed to appear for Governor and Matron.

So, what was the truth of the matter? Mr O'Brien must have realized that he had put himself in a difficult position. As he admits in his own letter, he had obtained from the Home Office permission to make 'a professional visit', yet he had turned up at the prison with his wife and all three of his children. Whilst his son was an articled clerk (trainee solicitor) and therefore entitled to be present at a professional visit, the others were clearly not – the governor was stretching a point in order to be humane to the prisoner in her last hours. It is pointless to speculate why Mr O'Brien chose to take his family with him. His younger daughter was in her early teens, an age which, in Victorian times, would have made it virtually inconceivable for the daughter of a professional man and non-relative of the prisoner to enter a condemned cell.

So, what made him so abusive to the prison staff? O'Brien was an Irish lawyer who had only recently established his practice in England[1] and had been instructed by the Irish community for the defence. We do not know what Kate Webster said to him in the whispered conversation. Was it that the English establishment had it in for 'us Irish' and she had been terribly treated? There are certainly indications in his letter that this is what happened.

2. The Problem with Kate

The reason why Kate Webster was awaiting her imminent death in Wandsworth Prison was that she had committed one of the most notorious murders by a female in the nineteenth century. She was, as a result, the only female of her generation whose case was featured in the *Notable British Trials* series. There were only two others in the series between 1850 and 1900: Madelyn Smith in Scotland and Florence Maybrick at the end of the century. Since among the editors of the series there were such great crime historians and commentators as William Roughhead and the barrister Filson Young, writing about her life should have been easy.

Unfortunately, the editor of Webster's trial, Elliott O'Donnell[2] (1872–1965), was an author known primarily for his books about ghosts. He claimed to have seen a ghost, described as an elemental figure covered with spots, when he was 5 years old. He also claimed to have been strangled by a mysterious phantom in Dublin. In later life, he became a ghost hunter, but first he traveled in America, working on a range in Oregon and becoming a policeman during the Chicago Railway Strike of 1894.

Returning to England, he worked as a schoolmaster and trained for the theatre. He served in the British army in the First World War, and later acted on stage and in movies. He specialized in what were claimed as true stories of ghosts and hauntings. These were immensely popular, but his flamboyant style and amazing stories suggest that he embroidered fact with a romantic flair for fiction. In addition to his more than fifty books, he wrote scores of articles and stories for national newspapers and magazines. He claimed 'I have investigated, sometimes alone, and sometimes with other people and the press, many cases of reputed hauntings. I believe in ghosts but am not a spiritualist.' Virtually every reference book in the field of supernatural fiction accords O'Donnell the status of a fiction writer.

His eighty-nine-page introduction to the trial, dwelling on Webster's background and early life, contains many risible touches, for example:

A record of her ancestry, which, unfortunately, it is impossible to obtain, would most likely show that some of them-in the not very remote past-were sheep stealers , cattle raiders and perhaps cattle maimers too; for there is no reason to suppose that the capacity for cruelty and barbarity is any the less inherent in us ... After all, practically everything that appertains to us is hereditary.

[Page 32 trial of Kate Webster] For Kate, despite the humbleness of her real position in life, was not common. The real Irish, no matter whether man or woman, no matter whether of the peasant class, or of the class just above the peasant, are never common it is not in their nature to be so; commonness is an attribute found only in those who are born and bred in a commercial nation.

The other problem is the destruction of almost all records relating to southern Ireland during the Irish Civil War, including marriages, deaths, and magistrates court and prison records. Fortunately, such records were available to the contemporary police investigating Mrs Thomas's murder, and for Webster's early life, we are dependent on these sources.

We know that Webster was born in Killane, a small village near Enniscorthy, Co., Wexford, Ireland in 1847. It was noted at her first trial in Liverpool that she had a Wexford conviction in December 1864 at the age of 17. Nothing is known about her immediate family, but after the murder of Mrs Thomas, she fled to Ireland where she was arrested in the village at the home of an uncle, a local farmer. It may be relevant that she was born at the height of the famine. County Wexford was not as badly affected as some other areas, but it still had a major impact on the county. Nicholas Furlong, illustrating the effects of the famine, states, 'In 1841 the population of County Wexford was 202,033. In 1851 it was 180,158, a drop of 21,875. The population continued to decline for the rest of the century.'

Among the myths, in the absence of evidence of Webster's early life, is that she stole money to pay for the boat fare to Liverpool and, according to her, while still a teenager, she married a Captain Webster and had four children by him. They were all deceased by the time she used the name.

3. A Professional Criminal

In December 1864, Webster was convicted of theft and sentenced to twelve months in Wexford Jail. By March 1866, she was in Liverpool, where she was convicted of stealing seven shirts, five nightgowns, three sheets, a pillow case and other assorted laundry, and sentenced to six months' imprisonment on 21 May. While we have no information on the circumstances of the theft, it seems clear by the list of stolen articles that she pretended to be a washerwoman or had stolen a bundle from a laundry.

Two years later, she was before the Liverpool borough sessions. The *Liverpool Daily Courier* of 15 February 1868, records that, on 14 February, under the name of Catherine Layles and described as a servant aged 21, she was convicted of stealing a dress on 30 January from the property of Joseph Connell and a dress and other articles on 20 December, the property of Elizabeth Down, being two of an organized series of lodging-house robberies, of which the prisoner had been found guilty.

In passing sentence, the recorder said that there were between twenty and thirty cases against the prisoner but, although she had previously been convicted, he could not send her to penal servitude for seven years as the conviction had not been proved. He would therefore sentence her to twelve months' imprisonment on the first indictment on which she been convicted, and five years' penal servitude on the second.

The April 1871 census lists 'Catherine Layless', aged 24 (evidence of having been born in 1847), occupation: domestic service, as an inmate of Knaphill female convict prison Woking, Surrey. This was a new prison, opened less than two years before when 100 women were transferred from Parkhurst Prison on the Isle of Wight. It is possible that Webster was among the first batch of prisoners transferred.

According to Webster, in her statement of 10 July 1879, she was released from the prison on 28 January 1872.

On release, she went to Mrs Meredith's home for discharged prisoners at Nine Elms Mission, Wandsworth Road, where she stayed for three months.

On 12 April 1875, she was arrested and charged with stealing a photographic album, a photograph, and other articles belonging to Frederick Clarke, stealing a scarf and other articles belonging to William Stockwell, and a shirt and other articles belonging to William Eastland, all at Kingston upon Thames. She was sentenced to eighteen months' hard labour in Wandsworth Prison.

On 18 January 1877, she was again arrested and charged with receiving a basket and a pair of cuffs, the property of Thomas Doran, at Kingston upon Thames. She was committed for trial and sentenced to twelve months' hard labour, again to be served in Wandsworth Prison.

4. The Murder Trial

On Wednesday, 2 July 1879, the trial of 'Kate Webster, alias Webb, alias Shannon, alias Lawless, alias Lawler for the murder of her mistress, Mrs Julia Martha Thomas, of two Vine cottages Park Road Richmond on about 2 March 1879', commenced.

The murder trial was unusual for its time in both its length and complexity. It lasted six working days during which fifty-three witnesses gave evidence. By contrast, Calvert's trial had one working day for its nineteen witnesses, and Mrs Willis's trial, with its complicated facts, only one day for the evidence.

The aim of the prosecuting barrister in any contested criminal trial, then as now, is to tell a convincing story by taking the jury through the evidence, so that they are sure that all the elements of an offence are present and it was committed by the defendant. In Webster's case, the basic details of the victim's disappearance, the theft of her property and the flight of the defendant to Ireland in order to avoid arrest were easy to prove, so would have, like the other two trials, resulted in a short trial. Even the absence of the body, as such, was easily accounted for by straight evidence of the police surgeon on the bones and other remains, and the linking of the bag thrown off Richmond Bridge in Webster's presence and its gruesome contents. Several facts were proved at the trial.

Mrs Thomas was an elderly widow who lived alone at 2 Vine Cottages, Park Road, Richmond. She had a local reputation as being difficult for whom to work. As a result, when looking for a servant in January 1879, a friend, Miss Loder, recommended Webster as a 'cook-general', sometime around the end of January 1879. It is clear that Webster was most unsatisfactory, as she was given notice to end on 28 February 1879. The last entry in Mrs Thomas's diary was that Webster had requested to stay on and her request was granted.

On Saturday, 2 March, her neighbour, Mrs Ives, saw Mrs Thomas tending her garden. The following morning Mrs Thomas went to the Presbyterian service in the lecture hall on Hill Street, Richmond. In the evening, she went to the evening service, where she spoke to a fellow celebrant about the terrible argument she had had with her new servant. It was the last time anyone saw her.

Sometime that night, she was killed, mutilated and dismembered. Kate Webster proceeded to boil part of the body. At about 11.00 am on the Monday morning, William Thomas Deane, a coal merchant, called about his bill.

Webster set out for Twickenham, perhaps with the rest of the remains of Mrs Thomas, which were never found. In any event, a foot was found in the manure heap on an allotment plot, a leftover from the box and bag that surfaced later.

Sometime in the afternoon, there is evidence that she called at the 'Hole in the Wall', the Park Road pub near Mayfield. At around 8.00 pm, she returned to Mayfield where, it is probable she spent considerable time cleaning and tidying up. The following morning, she was certainly scrubbing away, since she was seen at one of the windows with her sleeves rolled up.

The afternoon of Tuesday, 4 March, at about 3.00 pm, dressed in one of Mrs Thomas's silk gowns, and wearing her gold watch and chain and several of her rings, she started off to visit the Porters, a family she knew, living at Hammersmith. She had not seen them for six years.

Her plan, as outlined in court, was to get away from Richmond and pass herself off as Mrs Thomas as long as need be. She needed to sell as much of the furniture and effects she could, and then, after misdirecting all those who knew her as Kate Webster, take refuge in her old home in Ireland.

It was clear that the most immediate need was to get rid of the bag containing bits of Mrs Thomas. She took it with her to the Porters. She greeted Henry Porter, warmly sat down to tea, and told the Porters that, since seeing them last, she had married Mr Thomas. She added that he was now dead, and that her aunt had recently died too, leaving her a nice house in Richmond with all the personal effects. She told them that she was going to her parents in Scotland. Her dress and jewellery helped in the deception. It was clear that the Porter family swallowed the story. Webster asked Porter if he could recommend her an honest broker who would pay her a fair figure for the furniture at 2 Vine Cottages. As the author of the *Notable British Trial* series on Kate Webster comments, 'It was a colossal error. Had she being content with what she got in jewellery, plate and money and bolted for New York, she might have escaped.' She would have had a nineteen days' start on the authorities.

She also got Robert Porter, the 15-year-old son of the house, to carry the bag containing the remains to Richmond station. Porter father and son set out for Hammersmith station, Robert carrying the bag. He described it as strangely heavy for such a small bag, about 15in. inches long, 9in. deep and weighing about 30lb. They stopped at a pub by Hammersmith Bridge, the 'Oxford and Cambridge', then went on to Hammersmith station, where Porter senior left them. Going on to Richmond, she entered Mayfield with Robert Porter and picked up a bag containing meat and vegetables. She then asked Porter to help her to carry the box to the other side of Richmond Bridge, where the friend to whom she had arranged to give it, would be awaiting her.

Leaving the house together, carrying the box between them, they set off down Mount Ararat Road. On the way down, Porter chafed his knuckles on the side he was carrying that missed a handle. Unluckily for Kate, this helped Porter identify the box, a key link of evidence at the trial.

They reached Richmond Bridge where, halfway across, they put the box down on the seat in one of the recesses of the bridge (there are recesses on either side of the centre arch). According to Porter, she said that this was the arranged meeting place, and that he should go back and wait for her. He did not, and although he could not see anything, he heard a splash in the water below. Again, according to his evidence, a gentleman passed by and peered over the side of the bridge for a moment, before he walked on. Directly after he had gone, Kate came hurrying along. She informed Porter that she had seen her friend and had given her friend the box. She asked Porter to go with her to Richmond station to see if he could catch the last train home. They missed the train.

Porter was in a hurry to get home, but Kate persuaded him to go back to Park Road. According to Porter's evidence, they spent the night together in one room.

In the morning, he set off with the bag containing the provisions. Later that morning, Wednesday, 5 March, Webster went to the Porters and stayed there overnight.

The following day, William, the Porters' elder son, went with her to Mayfield Cottages. The evidence given by various people on Webster's movements after she left Hammersmith with William Porter at 7.00 pm was confused. It is clear that she was in Mayfield Cottages early on the Friday morning, as Mrs Porter turned up at Mayfield with Webster's purse, which she had forgotten the night before. After a couple of hours, the two women returned to Hammersmith. Webster spent Friday night at the Porters. The following morning, she set out to call upon Mrs Crease who had been looking after her little boy for almost two months. Webster then went to Mayfield to meet Mr Porter, who had been invited to view the furniture as he was trying to interest a broker. They then both returned to Hammersmith where she stayed with the Porters for the weekend.

On Sunday, 9 March, John Church, proprietor of the 'Rising Sun', Rose Gardens, Hammersmith, met Webster for the first time. She was in the company of Mr and Mrs Porter, and William Anders introduced by Porter to him. He had already been informed that 'Mrs Thomas' wanted to dispose of her home. He told her he would make an offer for the furniture provided it suited him.

Church saw her again on Monday and on Tuesday, 11 March when he went to the Thomas house to inspect the furniture, staying for several hours. Church returned on five consecutive days. He was in Webster's company on Sunday, 16 March, with the Porters. On Monday, 17 March, she spent the day at Mayfield Cottages, superintending the packing of the furniture. On Tuesday, 18 March, both he and Porter were there, assisting in the removal. Mrs Ives, the next-door neighbour and landlord became suspicious, and Webster panicked. She threw the dresses she was taking into the van in her haste to get away. Later, in one of the dresses, a letter was found through which her real identity was proven. In the pocket of a dress left behind in the house was found a letter from her uncle in Ireland, which made Webster easy to find.

In her panic, she picked up her child from the Porters and left for her uncle in Ireland, where everyone knew her. Her capture was only a matter of time.

Meanwhile, Church did nothing until Friday, 21 March. In one of the dresses Kate had thrown into the van, Mrs Church found a letter from a Mr Menhennick with an address in Finsbury Park. Church went around to Mr Menhennick's the same evening with Mr Porter. The deception of the two Mrs Thomases was unravelled. Mr Menhennick communicated with Mrs Thomas's solicitor, Mr Hughes. Mr Hughes dispatched his brother to see Church at the interview. On Saturday, 22 March, Church told the solicitor's brother everything he knew. Church sent for Porter, who told Mr Hughes all he knew about Webster. All three then went off to the Richmond police station.

The local police inspector, after listening to what they had to say, took the whole party to Vine Cottage. While they did not see anything that evening, Church immediately went to a cupboard from which he produced a gold watch and chain. This was an immediate cause of suspicion and a major factor in his being arrested, charged and finding himself in the dock of Richmond Magistrates Court, together with Webster when she was eventually brought back from Ireland.

On Sunday, 23 March, Robert Porter identified the box in which the remains had been found. After the circulation of a wanted notice, she was arrested on 28 March at Killane, in the house of her uncle Mr Lawless.

So why did it take nearly a whole day for Solicitor General Sir Hardinge Giffarde KC to outline the case, and another working day for the trial judge, Mr Justice Denman, to sum up the case for the jury?

The case for the Crown was muddied by Webster's charismatic influence over males, coupled with acting ability, nerves of steel and a reckless ability to lie.

Webster was no beauty – there is no photograph available, but a number of court sketches were made. She was a plain woman. Commentators, after the nature of the charge was known and she had appeared in the magistrates' court, dwelt on her forbidding savage features. Six years before, a serial poisoner, Mary Ann Cotton, had been executed in Durham. Not only were the same comments made by the journalists of the time on her appearance, but court sketches also reflected this. A photograph of Cotton does exist, in which she looks like a worried sheep.

But one can rely on the police's description of her on their wanted poster:

'Wanted, for stealing plate, etc, and supposed murder of mistress, Kate, aged about 32, 5 foot 5 or 6 inches high; complexion sallow; slightly freckled; teeth rather good and prominent'. Madame Tussauds produced a waxwork image of her, on view for the first time at Baker Street on Easter Monday, 1879, when she was still alive. The model certainly does not account for her ability to attract men.

Her first statement, made to the investigating police after being brought back from her uncle's farm in Ireland, pictured herself as the innocent victim of old lover Church:

> I have known John Church for nearly 7 years; I first got acquainted when I was living two or three doors from Church's, at Porter's. He used to take me out to London to various public houses. I met him again some months ago, and he came to my mistresses house one night worse for drink. ... My mistress came home ... and she said, 'Kate don't you think I'm very late?' 'no, as I have company ... my brother, who was come to see me.' A few days after he came again into the house and during conversation I told him the mistress had no money in the house; he said 'couldn't we put the old woman out of the way?' I said, 'what you mean?' He said, 'O poison her.' I said 'you must do that yourself; I'll have nothing to do with that.' Church said 'we would have her things and go off to America together and enjoy it, as I'm getting tired of my old woman.' He left late in the evening.
>
> He came again on the Monday night, 3 March, and had tea with Mrs Thomas ... When I returned late in the evening I noticed the light was turned down. I knocked three times at the door; third time Church opened the front door, when I saw Mrs Thomas lying on the mat in the passage struggling and groaning, he said 'come in' ... I said 'whatever have you done?' He said 'never you mind: I have done for her, and if you say a word about it, I'll put this knife into you, up to the handle.' ... I said 'no John don't; I won't tell ... Shortly after we left the house together leaving Mrs Thomas there ... Church saw me in to Mrs Porters and I remained there for the night. I got up early the next morning went into Church's house. Church was there and beckoned me to go up the street. He said 'I can't get over to your house before 1 o'clock.' I said I should not go back to the house by myself. He had the keys of the front and side door ... I told him I wouldn't be down there before night. He told me where to meet him, the Richmond hotel over the bridge. I took the boy Porter with me and as I passed the hotel I saw Church inside ... I went inside and spoke to Church ... He then gave me the keys to the house and said I would go back to the house,

taking the boy with me and I should find the box in the back room which he had packed up, tied with cord. The boy was to assist me to bring it away ... We carried it to the Bridge. Church told me to let the boy Porter keep back and not see him when I went with the box but he would be there to see me. I took the box to the Bridge ... Church appeared ... I left, and heard a splash in the water. I joined the boy Porter at the foot of the bridge carrying a carpet bag which we had also bought from the house. We went to the railway station and found that the last train had gone. I said, 'you shall come home and sleep with me.' We both slept in one room.

About two days after, when I was cleaning up the scullery, I saw some blood on the carving knife. There was a meat saw hanging up by the fireside, but on that day I found it on a box in the scullery, quite clean. Since Mrs Thomas disappeared, Church, Porter, and his boy have been frequently at the house, Church directing me to order meat, as if it was for Mrs Thomas. It is been taken to his house, cooked, and eaten there, likewise to Porters. He called Porter in to value the goods and furniture in the house, and said to me, 'Don't you pay for the valuation; I'll pay him.' I paid several bills; he said 'never mind paying them, pay Mrs Ives the landlady to keep her quiet.' I went to pay her when they were removing the goods ... She refused to take the money and thought there was something wrong. I went back into the house and told Church ... He said 'I'll go out to Porter and say I think there is something wrong about this; don't move the things.' He came back and said 'you will have to clear out and go to your friends,' and I left soon after ... This was on Tuesday the 19th and I reach my uncle's house at Greenanne on the following Friday night. I wrote to Church, to his address in Hammersmith, telling him I had arrived home safely. Before leaving, it was partly arranged that I should remain at home for about three weeks, that he would send me money to come back with, and then we were to go to America.

I never laid a hand on Mrs Thomas and had nothing to do with murdering her but I knew Church had done it. All the money left in the house belonging to Mrs Thomas was a 5 pound note and 30 shillings. This note I changed at a Fishmongers in Richmond. Church and Porter were with me at the time. I intend to tell the whole truth, as I don't see why I should be blamed for what Church has done. I wouldn't accuse my greatest enemy of anything wrong, let alone a friend, which Church had been to me up till now.

Statement No. 2:

Mr Church wanted to know how to get the furniture away. I told him he could manage that as well as the other business. He then asked my consent to let Porter value the furniture, so as to have a witness; he (Porter) did value the furniture at £50, and Mr Church drew the receipt himself ... On the next evening we were sitting on the sofa in the front room. Porter was there, and another man; I don't know his name. Church told me to look after the furniture till he removed it. He suspected Porter of moving anything. He then gave me £10 in gold and called Porter's attention to it. I asked him why he wanted Porter to be acquainted with our conversation on the subject. He said 'to keep things on my side square.'

Porter and the other man went on to Hammersmith. But the same time Church and I remained till the last train; that was on the Saturday night the 15th. On Sunday we went on the water. On Monday, I've think about 11 or 12 o'clock, we reach down here [Richmond], and went home about 10:30 on Monday night. On Tuesday morning we left home at about 8 o'clock he bought a man with him to collect the furniture and get it ready for the vans ... The vans came at 6:30. As soon as Mrs Ives saw the furniture going out she came in and asked the Carman where the furniture was going to be taken, and he declined to answer her. I was in the front room of the time with Mr Church. He asked me who she was, and I told in the landlady; he told me not to show myself and he would go out until the man to stop bringing out the furniture, and then it would not be noticed.

He then returned into the house and came into the front room and asked me to go and see the landlady, and if she wanted the money for the rent he would give it to me to pay her. I asked him what I should say to the landlady. He replied, 'if she asked to see Mrs Thomas, say she will be here in a few days.' I then saw the landlady, and asked if she wished to speak to me. She said 'no I want to see Mrs Thomas.' I told her she was not at home. I asked if she wanted the rent; she said 'no; I want to know whether furniture is going to.' I told her it was going to Hammersmith. She then said 'I will see about that.' I went back and told Mr Church what she'd said, and he said, 'I thought she was going to inform the police;' he then said 'I have the agreement to produce and I'm not frightened you can get out of the way.' ... I then left and went to rose gardens and took my child away. I thought I had none of money to travel with so I went on to Mrs Church's ... She gave me a half sovereign in 10 shillings in silver, and I left the house. Church took the plate away on the Saturday before the Tuesday the furniture was to be removed. He was accompanied by me and Porter. We had £12 of beef on the leg of mutton, a pound of cheese, a pound of butter 4 pounds of sugar 1 pound of tea a quartern of flour, a pound of suet, pound of wax candles, and one cake; these were taken to churches and divided, church taking the beef and candles, Porter the leg of mutton, cheese butter sugar T flower suet cake. All I have now told you is quite true.

Statement No. 3:

On 2nd March, when Church pulled me into the house, I heard a cough in the back room, and I fell inside the front room door against the chiffonier, and upon recovering myself I saw Henry Porter standing on the mat the front room door. He said to Church, 'what is the matter with her?' Church said, 'oh should be all right in a minute.' Porter said, didn't you see me coming in after you?' I said 'no' he said, 'I was coming behind you for a long way.' I suspected he had not followed me, and I asked him 'what way did I come?' He said 'straight up the hill by the church.' I said 'no I came the cemetery way' he then said 'there was someone very much like you on ahead of me.' Church said, 'don't hesitate; you both got here somehow,' Porter said 'that's quite right, but I never saw anyone so much like in my life.' Church and Porter then went into the back room.

After about 20 minutes Porter came out; he turned to Church and said, 'Jack I'll go on a little before you.' Church said, 'we are all going now in a minute.' Porter said 'there'll be too much notice taken of us all going out together.' Porter then took his hat from off the front room table and said to Church, 'I suppose I'll see you at home tonight, and then we can talk about matters.' Porter left, and afterwards Church and me followed.

We went from Richmond to Shaftesbury Road station, and when we got to the 'Rising Sun' Rose Gardens, Church said 'they are shut up; but there, come in.' I said 'no I won't: it is too late.' Church answered 'no she wants to get home.' Church insisted that I should go in but I would not; he said 'perhaps Porter wants to see you.' I said 'he must see me when he comes home.' I then left Church; I did not see Porter that night. I went to Porter's house: the door was opened by me and I went into the front parlour and went to bed on the sofa. I heard Porter come in about half an hour after; he fastened the door went into the back room, which is called the kitchen. I have often slept at the same place, and have lodged at Porter's house for six months in 1873. Shortly afterwards I heard the handle of the door of the room where I was sleeping turn, but I dropped it on the inside I asked who was there, and Mr Porter spoke and said 'it is me Kate; I want to see you.' I told him I was undressed and should see me in the morning. He then said 'good night; I'll be going out at five and I'll call you.'

I saw Porter at 10 minutes past five in the morning; he said 'I must go to work today to keep things straight; will you go home to Richmond before I come home tonight? I'll be home at five.' I said 'it all depends perhaps I won't go them.' Porter said 'Church is going down but we won't go till after dinner.' I says 'where did you see Church so early?' He said 'I was there last night when you came home didn't you know that?' I said 'yes, Mrs Church said so.' He said 'Church and me has arrange matters,' and that 'I must see tonight if I can get off. I'll get off I'll not do over time.' He then went away to his work.

I stop their till 5 o'clock that day, Monday, 3 March, when Porter came home. I got the tea ready is Mrs Porter was the worse for drink. After having tea Porter said 'are you going down?' I said 'yes I think I'll go.' He said 'Church is to meet me at Hartley's. Isn't the boy going down with you Kate?' (Meaning his son Robert). I said, 'yes.'

The boy went to wash himself, and Porter said, 'don't let that boy know anything, only as little as you can.' Porter me and the boy then went down to Hammersmith. We went into a public house near the old railway station and had something to drink. This was about 7 o'clock and I said 'now we must get on if we are going to Richmond tonight.' We went to the new station, and finding we had some time to wait, Port said we might walk to the Shaftesbury Road. We done so, and when we got to the top of the Shaftesbury Road the boys said, 'ain't you going home now, father?' He (Porter) said yes, he would go and have another pint to himself and then he would go. Porter asked me to come into a public house with him, but I said 'no I'd lose the train if I do,' the boy was waiting for me and he hurried him on and said 'Kate will catch you in a minute.' Porter arranged that he would come on to Richmond by the next train. I said 'can't you come home by this train?' He said 'no I don't want the boy to know it. I don't suppose I'll see you any more to night.' We then parted and I went to Richmond with the boy.

I saw Church at Hartley's, the Richmond hotel. I told the boy to go on in front of me. I went in and saw Church there and spoke to him. I told him Porter was coming by the next train; he asked me to have something to drink, and I had some whiskey and water: he then gave me two keys one of the side door, and one of the glass door at the back of the house, and said, 'you'll find a small box in the back room on the ground floor, between the sofa and bookcase; it ain't very heavy. I think the boy and you can manage it ... I'll be there sometime before you and all wait here until Porter comes does the boy know his father is coming down?' I said 'no the boy suspects something,' he asked me on the train, 'what is there Kate between father you and Church?'

I left Church and the public house and join the boy up the street, and went to the house with him. We then went in through the side entrance round to the glass door and into the back room. I lit the lights and after stopping in the house a short time we left by way of the front door carrying between us the box mentioned by Church and a large carpet bag. I don't know what was in the box, the bag contained a large family Bible and seven other books, some meat and a number of things We carried the box all the way. Getting on the middle of the bridge we put the box down. I said to the boy 'now you get on to the station and I'll catch you' he said 'very well Kate' and went. Then Church came up to me, and I said to him 'how long have you been here?' He said 'not very long' I said 'where is Porter, did you see him?' He said 'yes I waited for him;

don't let the boy know we are here; go on after him as quick as you can;' I said 'where is the cab for this box? You can't carry it' he said 'never mind that I'll see about it' I then left Church and, following the boy I got a short distance away when I heard a splash in the water.

At the conclusion of every case under English law, it is for the judge to sum up the evidence fairly so that the jury can come to a conclusion on the facts. Mr Justice Denman observed during his course of his summary:

> The case was complicated by the fact that at three different times the accused had made three distinct statements all mentioning as facts a great number of circumstances as to every one of which it was important, in the interests of justice, that a full enquiry should be made. 53 witnesses have been called, every one of whom tended, if their evidence was accepted, to throw light upon the case. It was his duty to do what he could to assist them in coming to a true and just solution of this case ...
>
> The charge was one of murder, and they would have to say whether one person or another, or more than one person, committed that murder ... If they entertained any doubt whether Mrs Thomas was murdered or not, and whether the accused was concerned in the murder, it was their duty to acquit the accused.
>
> They could not expect that in such a prosecution is this, every witness should be a choice or select one. There would be witnesses with weak points, and it would be for the jury to say how far they accepted or discredited the evidence of these witnesses ... Sometimes there would be discrepancies between witnesses, especially where dates were involved or circumstances or conversations or as to who were or who were not present on certain occasions ... In such a case as this, he supposed they would always lean to the side which told most favourably towards the accused.
>
> Three statements had been made by the prisoner which were long and intricate. The jury ought to look at them as a whole, and see whether they did fairly or not consist with the facts proved in the case ... There were two portions of the accused statement as to the date of certain events afterwards altered to another date. It was for them to say whether they were made in full knowledge of their

importance. They ought to have an irresistible conviction that the accused was guilty before finding her guilty and there was no reasonable prospect of her innocence. The learned counsel for the defence had argued that this was not conclusively made out, and had pointed out the various heads upon which he relied upon making that proposition. He said that the box found upon the model of the Thames on the morning of 5 March was not conclusively proved to contain the remains of Martha Thomas ... If a multitude of circumstances so combined that to hold otherwise would be contrary to common sense, they were bound not to violate common sense. They would not be justified in taking each individual circumstantial evidence as it existed alone and to the contrary get doubts as to whether the thing also to be proved would be proved by one fact alone. According to the accused's own statement, there was Mrs Thomas dead in the house, and according to the evidence of the police and others, human remains were found in the house ... Then two or three days after the death of Mrs Thomas boiled human remains mixed, in one instance with a portion of a human body which had not been boiled, were found on the banks of the Thames. These were a woman's remains, which might be believed to be those of a person was missing in that neighbourhood upon that time, as Mrs Thomas appeared to have been; and they were found in a box identified by two witnesses. The accused also mentioned the carrying of a box, and taking it all together was there any reasonable doubt left the box was taken from the house, and that the remains were those of Mrs Thomas?

The next point suggested was that it must be shown beyond all possible doubt that she did not die from natural causes. They had to think of all the circumstances, and one was that the accused twice alluded to something like a violent death, because she first said that Church had told her he had 'done it' and subsequently she said 'I know nothing about the death. I had no hand in murdering her, but I know that he did it' coupling these statements with the statement relating to the quantity of blood was inconceivable ... Mrs Thomas came to her death by natural causes, and not by violence.

The judge then dealt in terms with the evidence that might have implicated Porter, or Church.

Having touched upon the main topics of the views taken on one side or the other, his lordship proceeded to go through the evidence with regard to what was going on with respect to Mrs Thomas herself, the accused, the Porters, Church, and the other persons who bore a part in the story from the first material time down to the last material time in the case. He continued:

> It was in controversy whether the accused knew Church until 9 March. One thing was clear, and that was that, down to 9th March, Church was the master of his public house, and he produced testimonials that he was a man of good character. Mrs Thomas was a lady of 54 years of age, of middle height, healthy and strong, as far as could be seen from the photograph, and the accused had called her a good living woman. Porter seems to have been a hard-working man, but his wife was a miserable drunkard. The boy Porter had given his evidence tolerably straightforwardly; but in his cross examination he used one form of expression 'might or might not be' which was peculiar, showing that he was cautious.

The jury took just over an hour to find Webster guilty. Webster pleaded she was with child and went through the panel of matrons' procedure. She was not.

Kate also produced a lengthy autobiographical statement in the form of a confession to her Covent Garden solicitor, Fitzroy O'Brien, in the death cell at Wandsworth. She could not read or write. It is to be found in her Home Office death file, which was opened to the public in 1990.

Kates autobiography:

> Her Majesty's prison at Wandsworth.
> Thursday, July 10, 1879.
> Statement of Catherine Webster, now a prisoner under sentence of death for the murder of Mrs Thomas at Richmond on 2 March 1879 as follows:
> I make this statement in the first place, merely thanking my solicitor, Mr O'Brien, who has defended me at the police court and upon my trial at the Central criminal Court and to whom I owe a debt of gratitude for the interest he has taken in my behalf under difficulties most trying to him and to myself and for all that he has done for me. I tend my heartfelt thanks and gratitude also to my counsel, Mr Sleigh and Mr Keith, for the attention they

had given to my case. In the first place, I am advised that I ought not to be found guilty upon the evidence, which was wholly circumstantial, and also upon the plea I have pleaded.

I was born at Killane, in the county of Wexford and am about 30 years of age. I left home in Ireland about the year 1867 and came to England. I got into trouble in Liverpool upon my arrival and got five years penal servitude on 13 February 1868. I was discharged on 28 July 1872.

When I got my discharge I went to Mrs Meredith's Home for discharged prisoners at Nine Elms where I remained three months. I then got a situation through Mrs Meredith at Grove Road Wandsworth where I remained three or four months and left of my own accord. Upon leaving there I went to live to Porter's house in number 10 Rose Gardens Hammersmith. I knew the Porters through a fellow prisoner named Carr, who introduced me to them. I lodged with Carr, about five doors from Church's, and afterwards went to live next door to Porter's. I was living in Porter's house for six months and what he has sworn respecting this was wholly false. At this time I was in the habit of going out washing with Mrs Porter, a woman named Lizzie was living at the time at number 10 Rose Gardens and used to do Mrs Smith's washing at number 10. I became very much attached to Porter's family and they were also very much attached to me From there I went to Captain Woolbest's, Royal Crescent Notting Hill as Cook and housemaid. I used to visit Mrs Marsh close to and made Strong's acquaintance while there.

A charge of felony was made against Mr Marsh and Strong came up to bail him out. Strong at this time was living in Holloway and kept an oil shop. I was induced by him to go to live with him at his house and he seduced me while there and got me in the family way of my little boy now about six years old. Strong at this time obtained some goods from America by foul means. The goods consisted of a number of tanks. I assisted him in doing so and was of obliged to leave Holloway and go to live at Kingston. He induced me to live with him at Kingston, and took a room, for me at number 5 acre Road, where my boy was born on April 19, 1874. I went from there to London Street [Windman's Cottage] for which Strong was to pay four shillings and sixpence a week and he left me there to do the best I could to keep myself and child. I became very impoverished forsaken by him, and committed crimes for the purpose of supporting myself and child. I could not get a place to leave the child and was open to all kinds of temptation. I was charged with three offences of stealing at Kingston and sentenced to 18 months hard Labour on 14 April 1875. I was but a short time at my liberty and on 18 January 1877, was sentenced to 12 months imprisonment of the Surrey sessions on 6 February 1877. I was innocent of that charge ...

In view of the seriousness of the crime, the Crown was led by Solicitor General Sir Hardinge Gifford. Webster was defended by Mr. Warner Sleigh.

A hat maker named Mary Durden gave evidence for the prosecution, telling the court that on 25 February, Webster had told her she was going to Birmingham to take control of the property, jewellery, etc., that had been left her by a recently deceased aunt. This, the prosecution claimed, was clear evidence of premeditation, as the conversation had occurred six days before the murder.

One of the problems of the prosecution case, however, was proving that the human remains the police had found were actually those of Mrs Thomas. It was a weakness that her defence sought to capitalize on, especially as, without the head, there was no means of positively identifying them at that time. Medial evidence was given to show that all the body parts had belonged to the same person and that they were from a woman in her fifties. The defence tried to suggest that Mrs Thomas may have died of natural causes, in view of her agitated state, when she was last seen alive leaving church on the Sunday afternoon.

Both Henry Porter and John Church gave evidence against Webster, describing the events of which they had been involved. Her defence again tried to point the finger of suspicion at them. In his summing up, the judge, however, pointed to the actions and previously known good characters of both of them. Two of Webster's friends, Sarah Crease and Lucy Loder, gave evidence of her good nature.

Late on the afternoon of Tuesday, 8 July, the jury retired to consider their verdict. Returning just over an hour later, they pronounced her guilty.

Before she was sentenced, Webster yet again made a complete denial of the charge, but cleared Church and Porter of any involvement in the crime. As was normal, she was asked if she had anything to say before she was sentenced, to which she claimed to be pregnant. She was examined by a panel of matrons drawn from some of the women present in the court, who dismissed this claim as just another of her lies. She went back to Newgate, before being transferred the next day to Wandsworth to await execution.

It has been suggested that Wandsworth did not have a condemned cell at this time, although it would seem unlikely. In any event, Webster was guarded around the clock by teams of female prison officers.

Webster was to make two further 'confessions' in Wandsworth, the first implicating Strong, who was the father of her child. These allegations were also found to be baseless. Webster was informed by her solicitor that no reprieve was to be granted to her, despite a small amount of public agitation for commutation. So, on the eve of her hanging, Webster made another confession to the solicitor in the presence of the Catholic priest attending her, Father McEnrey. Seeming somewhat nearer the truth, she stated that she was resigned to her fate and that she would almost rather be executed than return to a life of misery and deception.

The actual execution of the sentence of death had changed a great deal over the eleven years between the ending of public hangings and Webster's death, even though the words of the sentence had not. No longer was it a public spectacle, with the prisoner being given a short drop and allowed to die in agony. William Marwood had made great improvements to the process, by introducing the 'long-drop' method, designed to break the person's neck and cause instant unconsciousness.

The execution was, as usual, to take place three clear Sundays after sentence, and was set for the morning of Tuesday, 29 July at Wandsworth Prison. Wandsworth was originally the Surrey House of Correction and had been built in 1851. It took over the responsibility for housing Surrey's condemned prisoners on the closure of Horsemonger Lane Gaol in 1878.

Webster was to be only the second person and the sole woman to be hanged there.

At 8.45 am, the prison bell started to toll. A few minutes before 9.00 am, the undersheriff, the prison governor, Captain Colville, the prison doctor, two male warders and Marwood formed up outside her cell. Inside, Webster was being ministered to by Father McEnrey and attended by two female wardresses. She would have typically been offered a stiff tot of brandy before the execution commenced. The governor entered her cell and told her that it was time. She was led out between the two male warders, accompanied by Father McEnrey, across the yard to the purpose-built execution shed, which was nicknamed the 'Cold Meat Shed'.

Having the gallows in a separate building spared the other prisoners from the sound of the trapdoor falling, and made it easier too for the staff to deal with the execution and removal of the body afterwards. As Webster entered the shed, she would have been able to see the large white-painted gallows with the rope dangling in front of her, its simple noose laying on the trapdoors. The idea of coiling up the rope to bring the noose to chest level came later, as did the brass eyelet in the noose. Marwood stopped her on the chalk mark on the double trapdoors. He placed a leather body-belt round her waist to which he secured her wrists, while one of the warders strapped her ankles with a leather strap. She was not pinioned in her cell, as became the normal practice later. She was supported on the trap by the two warders standing on planks (one is just visible in the bottom left hand corner of the photo) set across it. This had been the normal practice for some years in case the prisoner fainted or struggled at the last moment. Marwood placed the white hood over her head and adjusted the noose, leaving the free rope running down her back.

Her last words were, 'Lord, have mercy upon me.'

He quickly stepped to the side and pulled the lever, Webster plummeting down some eight feet into the brick-lined pit below. Marwood used significantly longer drops than were later found to be necessary.

Webster's body was left to hang for the usual hour before being taken down and prepared for burial. The whole process would have taken around two minutes in those days, considered vastly more humane than Calcraft's executions.

The black flag was hoisted on the flag pole above the main gate, where a small crowd of people had gathered for her execution. They would have seen and heard nothing, yet these rather pointless gatherings continued outside prisons during executions until abolition. As the criminal was female, no newspaper reporters had been allowed to attend the execution. The *Illustrated Police News*, however, did one of their famous drawings of the scene as they imagined it, with Marwood putting the hood over a pinioned Webster's head.

William Marwood received £11 for hanging Webster, presumably £10 plus £1 expenses.

Later in the day, her body was buried in an unmarked grave in one of the exercise yards at Wandsworth. Nobody else was to be buried in this grave, although after the ninetieth execution, the authorities started to re-use male graves, but not hers.

What had actually happened?

On 13 January 1879, Webster entered the service of Mrs Julia

Martha Thomas at No. 2 Vine Cottages, Park Road, Richmond. To begin with, the two women got on well. Webster recorded that she felt she could be happy working for Mrs Thomas, who was comfortably off, although a rather eccentric woman in her mid-fifties. Soon, however, the poor quality of Webster's work, and her frequent visits to local pubs, began to irritate Mrs Thomas. After various reprimands, she gave Webster notice with her dismissal to take effect on Friday, 28 February. This period of notice was a fatal mistake on the part of Mrs Thomas. She had become increasingly frightened of her employee during this period, so much so that she asked friends from her church and relatives to stay in the house with her.

Friday the 28th arrived, and as Webster had not managed to find a new job or any accommodation, she pleaded with Mrs Thomas to be allowed to remain in her house over the weekend. Sadly, Mrs Thomas agreed to this, a decision that was to cost both women their lives.

On the Sunday morning, 2 March 1879, Mrs Thomas went off to church as usual. Webster was allowed Sunday afternoons off work, but had to be back in time for Mrs Thomas to go to the evening service. This Sunday afternoon, Webster went to visit her son, who was as usual in the care of Sarah Crease, before going to a pub on the way back to Vine Cottages. Thus, she got back late, which inconvenienced Mrs Thomas, who again reprimanded her before rushing off so as not be late for the service. Fellow members of the congregation noticed that she seemed agitated. Whether this was because she suspected Webster's dishonesty and feared her home was being robbed, is quite possible. Whatever the reason, Mrs Thomas left church before the end of the service and went home, sadly without asking anyone to accompany her. Precisely what happened next is unclear.

In her confession prior to her execution, Webster described the events:

> We had an argument which ripened into a quarrel, and in the height of my anger and rage I threw her from the top of the stairs to the ground floor. She had a heavy fall. I felt that she was seriously injured and I became agitated at what had happened, lost all control of myself and to prevent her screaming or getting me into trouble, I caught her by the throat and in the struggle choked her.

At her trial, the prosecution painted a rather different picture.

Mrs Thomas's next door neighbour, Mrs Ives, heard the noise of the fall, followed by silence. At the time, she thought no more of it. Little was she to suspect what was to happen next. Webster, of course, now had the problem of what to do with the body. Instead of just leaving it and escaping, however, she decided to dismember it and then dispose of the parts in the river. She set about this grim task with a will, firstly cutting off the dead woman's head with a razor and meat saw, before hacking off her limbs. She parboiled the limbs and torso in a copper pot on the stove and burned Mrs Thomas' organs and intestines. Even Webster was revolted by all this and the enormous amount of blood everywhere. She stuck to the job, however, systematically burning or boiling all the body parts and then packing the remains into a wooden box, except for the head and one foot, for which she could not find room. It has been said that Webster even tried to sell the fatty remains from boiling the body as dripping.

Mrs Ives was later to report a strange smell from next door, which had been caused by the burning. Webster disposed of the spare foot on a manure heap, but was left with the problem of the head. This she decided to place into a black bag.

She continued to clean up the cottage on the Monday and Tuesday, before 'borrowing' one of Mrs Thomas's silk dresses and visiting the Porter family on the Tuesday afternoon, taking the black bag containing the head with her. She told the Porters that she had benefited under the will of an aunt who had left her a house in Richmond. She wanted to dispose of the house, together with its contents, as she had decided to return to Ireland. She asked Henry Porter if he knew of a property broker who might be able to assist her.

Later in the evening, Webster excused herself and went off, ostensibly to visit another friend, returning later without the black bag, which was never found. Both Henry Porter and his son Robert had carried the bag for Webster at various stages of their walk to the railway station and two pubs along the way, both noticing how heavy it was.

This left Webster with the rest of the human remains in the box of which to dispose. She sought the services of young Robert Porter to help her in this, taking the lad back home with her for the purpose. She and Porter carried the box between them to Richmond Bridge, where Webster said she was meeting someone who was taking the box. She told Porter to go on without her. Porter was to hear a splash of something heavy hitting the water below a few moments before Webster caught up with him again.

The box was discovered the next morning by a coal man, who must have had a horrible shock when he opened it. He reported his discovery to Inspector Harber at Barnes police station.

The police had the various body parts examined by a local doctor, who declared that they were from a human female. He noticed that the skin showed signs of having been boiled. Without the head, however, it was not possible to identify the body.

Webster, meanwhile, was calling herself Mrs Thomas, even wearing the dead woman's clothes and jewellery. She kept up pressure on Henry Porter to help her dispose of the property. He introduced her to a Mr John Church, a publican and general dealer, who she persuaded to buy the contents of the house. Webster and Church seemed to rapidly become friends and went drinking together several times. The real Mrs Thomas had not been reported missing at this stage. The newspapers referred to the human remains in the box as 'the Barnes Mystery', a fact known to Kate as she could read – as could the Porter family. Robert Porter told his father about the box that he had helped Webster carry, which was like the one described in the papers.

Webster agreed to a price for the furniture and some of Mrs Thomas's clothes with Church and he arranged for their removal. Unsurprisingly, this was to arouse the suspicion of Mrs Ives next door, who questioned Webster as to what was going on. Mrs Church was later to find a purse and diary belonging to Mrs Thomas in one of the dresses. There was also a letter from a Mr Menhennick, to whom Henry Porter and John Church paid a visit. Menhennick knew the real Mrs Thomas, and it became clear from the discussion that it could well be her body in the box. The three men, together with Menhennick's solicitor, went to the Richmond police station to report their suspicions. The next day a search was made of No. 2 Vine Cottages, where an axe, a razor and some charred bones were recovered, together with the missing handle from the box found in the river. Thus, on 23 March, a full description of Kate Webster was circulated by the police in connection with the murder of Mrs Thomas and the theft of her effects.

Webster had decided to flee to Ireland, taking her son with her. This was to be the first place the police looked for her. She was arrested on 28 March, and kept in custody awaiting collection by two detectives from Scotland Yard. She was brought back to England and taken to Richmond police station, where she made a statement on 30 March 30th and formally charged with the murder. The statement accused John Church of being responsible for Mrs Thomas's death. He was subsequently arrested and also charged with the murder. Fortunately, he had a strong alibi and had also assisted the police in discovering the crimes. At the committal hearing, the charges against him were dropped, while Webster was remanded in custody.

If the events of that Sunday evening were exactly as Webster had described them, it is strange that Mrs Ives did not hear the quarrel or any other noises from next door. Again, why were there bloodstains at the top of the stairs if Mrs Thomas's injuries had occurred at the bottom? It is generally held that Webster lay in wait for Mrs Thomas. She hit her on the head with an axe, causing her to fall down the stairs, where she then strangled her to prevent any further noise. This would, of course, make the crime one of premeditated murder, which is much more in line with the forensic evidence. Whether Kate decided to kill Mrs Thomas in revenge for her earlier telling off or whether it was because she saw a great opportunity to steal from Vine Cottages, or both, is unclear.

It was reported in October 2010 that Julia Martha Thomas's skull had finally been discovered in the grounds of Sir Richard Attenborough's property in Park Road, Richmond, by workmen excavating for an extension. Attenborough had purchased a former pub, the 'The Hole in the Wall', which was adjacent to his property, and had demolished the rear of the pub. It is highly likely that Kate Webster frequented 'The Hole in the Wall'. The coroner's report stated that the skull had fractures consistent with falling down stairs. It also had depleted collagen, which suggested that it had been boiled.

Was Kate Webster the first 'Thames Torso' murderess?

It was Elliot O'Donnel's love of gossip that put me on the trail of further possible offences by Webster. O'Donnell's wide-ranging observations in the introduction included a reference to the Thames Torso mystery. Added to this, his own careful chronology, on pages 7–8[1], of Webster's terms in prison, demonstrate that she was free and living by the Thames. Also, on page 70:

> It has been stated on reliable authority that father McEnery told a friend of his Catherine Webster's confession was the most horrible narrative effects that in all his experience of prison life he had listened to; and from one who knew him I learnt that the recital of these facts made such an impression on him that he was never the same man afterwards.

Four years after the publication of the trial of Kate Webster, O'Donnell wrote another book, *Great Thames Mysteries*[2], in which he remarks on the Thames Torso murders in general, with the Salamanca Place murderer possibly the fiend responsible for them. It is, I think, generally agreed that one person did them all. He had all the clues but for some reason failed to connect the dots.

Between May 1887 and September 1889, no fewer than six discoveries of parts of dismembered women's corpses were discovered in the Thames, all of which had been decapitated. They are known as the Thames Torso murders and the identity of only one of the women was ever established. However, there were two earlier murders involving body parts and decapitation of women in 1873 and 1874.

On 4 September 1873, the Thames police discovered the left quarter of a female torso floating in the river near Battersea. Over the ensuing weeks, body parts were found floating or stranded in Woolwich, Greenwich, and near Wandsworth Bridge. The consensus of opinion was that the body parts had entered the Thames just west of Wandsworth Bridge. Then a body part was found on 11 September, when a foot was found floating in the river off Hammersmith. There was an inquest, frequently adjourned, which eventually found that the parts belonged to a woman about 40 years old. There was speculation that the woman was a recently released convict, still sporting her prison haircut, the hair very dark, very thin and somewhat short. Eventually, eleven body parts were found.

There was a *Times* editorial on 16 September, which summed it up:

'The facts point to a murder of a character more than usually atrocious; but the remains of not hitherto been identified literally nothing to guide suspicion to the place where the murder was perpetrated. Not a particle of the dead woman's clothing has been found'.

Neither murderer nor victim were ever identified.

Very little is known about a female body found in the Thames at Putney in June 1874. The *News of the World* of 14 June carried the story of a headless body without arms, but with one leg remaining, that was taken from Putney riverbank to Fulham Union Workhouse. At the subsequent inquest, Dr E.C. Barnes, a police surgeon, stated that he believed the body had been divided, and a covering of lime used to aid decomposition.

The leading book, of only two recent ones on these murders, is M.J. Trow's *The Thames Torso Murders*[3]. Here there is an attempt to link the two groups together as being performed by one serial killer, familiar with London slaughterhouses.

One must ask the question as to why, with a gap of over a decade to account for the theory of two separate serial killers, had received such little attention.

Stripped to its essentials, Kate Webster murdered a woman, the body was dismembered and parts thrown into the Thames in 1879.

Her own personal history discloses, at the end of January 1872, that she was released from a long spell of imprisonment, during which time she was moved from Leeds to a prison in Weybridge. From there, she had entered a home for released prisoners at Nine Elms, just south of the river and near Wandsworth.

Around the time of the first murder, Webster was living in Kingston, upriver from Putney. She was constantly visiting her friends, the Porters, at 10 Rose Gardens, Hammersmith, probably near the river – the exact location is now unknown. She was still at liberty at the time of the second murder, having given birth to her son in September 1874. The rest of her life saw her in and out of local prisons with very little time at liberty.

A possible narrative in favour of Kate Webster as the first Tow-Path Torso murderess, might go as follows:

A considerable number of the 'friends' she must have made in the women's prison and in the borstel would have been prostitutes. As a generality, prostitutes worked in the streets. If they were successful on a night, they would carry their money with them. Webster would know their habits, for example where they went drinking after a night's work. During this time, she was either working as a cook-general or live-in housekeeper. She had access to the Porter's kitchen, in which she could have practised the butchery on these earlier victims that she was proven to have employed in dealing with Mrs Thomas. It was also proven at Webster's trial that Porter was a hard-working man (out all day?), but his wife was a miserable drunkard (out in another sense), leaving the coast clear.

The case against Kate Webster is founded on these strands of being in the general vicinity of the murders. She was the only known practitioner of this type of murder of the times, and this earlier series stopped abruptly due to regular incarcerations ending with her execution in 1878. One applies the duck test. Indiana poet James Whitcomb Riley (1849–1916) may have coined the phrase when he wrote, 'When I see a bird that walks like a duck and swims like a duck and quacks like a duck, I call that bird a duck'.

The analogy is that when one finds two duck eggs on the lawn, and there is only one duck in the garden, then that duck laid the egg. Two dismembered bodies are found in the Thames during the only period other than months in Kate Webster's adult life, when she was not only at liberty, but living in the general vicinity of the Thames. On this basis, it is quite likely that Webster was responsible for the early Thames Torso murders.

Part 4
'Mrs Willis'

Timeline

1887
Birth of Emma Willis junior.

1888
| 13 July | Marriage (1) under the name Emma Dalzell to Thomas Willis, Sunderland. |

1893   Arrives in Cardiff?
8 April   Marriage (2) between the same parties, Cardiff.

1893–1896
The couple have two daughters.

1896
Putative death of Thomas Willis.
Thomas Willis's relatives take away the two younger daughters, leaving Emma Jr with Emma.

1896–1901
Co-habits with Stewart MacPherson in Cardiff and Bootle.

1897
Dorothy MacPherson born.

1900
Bessie MacPherson born.

1901
| April | Living with Gregor MacPherson, under the name Rhoda McPherson, with the two daughters. |

| 1903 | Living with Robert Carew, a blacksmith. |

1906
| June | Leaves Robert Carew. |
| 16 July | Is arrested on charge of stealing landlord's property under the name of Rhoda Willis, and sentenced to one calendar months' hard labour, Cardiff. |

August 1906–May 1907
Lives with David Evans a bootmaker in Pontypool.

1907

March   Rhoda Willis places an advert for a baby to adopt
                 in *The Evening Press*. Advert leads to adoption of
                 baby Stroud, and other babies, including baby
                 Treasure.

20 March   Baby Stroud born and handed over to 'Leslie
                 James'.

May   Baby Stroud is dumped on Salvation Army
                 doorsteps, and dies eight days later.

3 June   Baby Treasure born.

4 June   'Leslie James' travels to Hengoed railway station.
                 Collects baby Treasure and smothers it on the
                 railway journey home.

5 June   Landlady discovers baby Treasure dead near
                 Willis's bed. She calls police who immediately
                 charged her with murder.

23–24 June   Trial of 'Leslie James' at Swansea Assize. Found
                 guilty and sentenced to death.

14 August   Execution of Mrs Willis at Cardiff Prison.

1911

April   Thomas Willis In Cardiff Workhouse.

1917

15 March   Death of Thomas Willis at sea.

1. The Last Confession

Harold M. Lloyd had been dreading his last appointment of the
day as he pressed the entrance doorbell of Cardiff Prison on 13
August 1907. The portly 29-year-old solicitor had drawn up his
client Rhoda Willis's will, and had brought it for her to sign and
be witnessed by the matrons looking after her. A lifelong opponent
of capital punishment, he anticipated a harrowing interview with
her, since he thought it was the last meeting she would have with
anyone before the execution scheduled to take place at 8.00 am the
following morning.

He was surprised at the welcome he received from the waiting
warden, but as the conversation began, it was clear that he was the
victim of mistaken identity. He was not interested in having his tea
and being conducted to the gallows. The warden had mistaken him
for one of the Pierrepoint brothers due to arrive at the same time,
and expected him to join his brother in testing the drop before the

morning ceremony. Later, the warden had a hearty laugh about his mistake with the waiting journalists.

Mr Lloyd was not amused. All the officials he encountered on the way noted his agitation and distress. He arrived in the condemned cell to see the woman he knew as Mrs Leslie James in a state of collapse. It took some time to revive her sufficiently for him to deal with business. She left what little she had to Mr Macpherson to help him care for their daughters.

It was only then that she revealed to Mr. Lloyd that her real name was Rhoda Willis, having been charged, tried and convicted in the assumed name of Leslie James. Apparently, her motive for this deceit was to avoid bringing shame on her family, according to the *Western Mail* newspaper[1].

She was, so the paper reported, been born Rhoda Leselles. She must have told Mr Lloyd it was Dalziel. but in his distress, he misheard. She was originally from Sunderland, and had been given a good education at a girls' boarding school in London. Around the age of 19, she met and later married Thomas Willis, a marine engineer from Sunderland. The couple moved to the Grangetown area of Cardiff, where Willis gave birth to a daughter.

Thomas later died of natural causes, leaving Willis on her own to bring up their child. She took up with a Mr E.S. Macpherson, strangely, another marine engineer. The couple lived together for some time in Paget Street, Cardiff, with Willis bearing him two daughters before they decided to separate. Willis went to live with her brother in Birmingham, while the two children stayed with their father. She later returned to Cardiff, where she had begun to drink heavily and was generally going 'down hill'.

In 1907, she was knocked down by a bicycle. She sustained a head injury, which necessitated a lengthy stay in the workhouse infirmary. After her release, she was convicted of her first criminal offence, the theft of a medal, for which she received a short prison sentence.

This 'deathbed' confession was in fact a tangled web of truths, half-truths and downright falsehoods. Mysteries still remain.

2. The Problem with Mrs Willis

We only have four recorded documents relating to Mrs Willis: two marriage certificates, an entry in the 1901 census, and a death certificate. The rest is from three police reports to the Home Office and in the death file which, in turn, were based on local gossip and some statements. What we can tell from modern investigation is that Mrs Emma – never Rhoda – Willis was a consummate liar about herself and her immediate family. It is clear that her eldest child, Emma, was unlikely to be the daughter of her husband, Thomas, although she lived out her long life in the belief that she was.

The sort of mess that this woman of 'loose morals', according to the standards of her time left behind her, can be illustrated by the third police report from the chief constable of Cardiff to the Home Office, dated 8 August 1907 – six days before her execution. (See below) It informed the Home Office of the disputed paternity of her last two children.

3. The Murder and the Trial

Willis placed an advert for a baby to adopt in *The Evening Press* and gave a post office box number to reply to. One was received from a Mrs Lydia English, whose sister Maude Treasure was pregnant. It was agreed that Leslie James, as Mrs English knew her, would take the baby when it was born, which it duly was on 3 June 1907. Willis collected the infant the following day. She paid the pre-agreed fee of £8 at Hengoed railway station, before taking her by train back to her lodgings at Portmanmoor Road, Splott, in Cardiff. It was on this train journey, she later confessed, that she smothered the baby. Willis wrote out a receipt for the money and Lydia and Maude had kept it. She had also written another letter to Lydia English after the baby's death, in which she said, 'I am leaving for the North. Have just given baby a nice bath. She is lovely.'

Willis also received other replies to her advertisement, including one from an Emily Stroud from Abertillery, who had had a baby on 20 March 1907. Willis took this child and kept it until early May, when she dumped it outside the Salvation Army House in Cardiff, with a note claiming she was an unmarried mother who could not cope. Sadly, the baby was not discovered quickly enough and subsequently died eight days later from exposure. Another child was adopted on 8 May, but this one was able to return to its parents unharmed.

Her landlady, Mrs Wilson, told the police that Willis had gone out on 5 June and had returned home drunk. She helped to get her to bed and noticed a bundle by the bed. When she opened it, she was horrified to find the body of a newborn baby girl. She immediately sent for the police who arrested Willis at the scene. She was charged with murder and remanded in custody to the next Glamorgan Assizes.

She was tried at Swansea before Mr Commissioner Shee on Tuesday and Wednesday, 23 and 24 June 1907, on the one charge of murder of Maude Treasure's unnamed baby. She pleaded not guilty and claimed that the child had been ill and therefore died of natural causes. Examination of the baby showed that it had been dead for between twelve and forty-eight hours when it had been discovered, but had been healthy at birth. The prosecution showed that she had died from asphyxia, having been smothered, although the defence claimed that the suffocation could have been accidental. This might well have been accepted and led to an acquittal, had it not been for the letter that Willis had sent after the baby's death.

Handwriting experts claimed that the writing on the note, found with the dumped baby outside the Salvation Army House, was Willis's, as it matched the writing in a letter sent by her to Lydia English and the receipt for the £8. The jury retired at 2.45 pm on the second day of the trial, taking just twelve minutes to bring in a verdict of guilty.

Commissioner Shee agreed with their verdict and told Rhoda:

> Don't let anyone suppose that because you are convicted of murder that nobody pities you, nobody prays for you. I implore you to employ the short time that is left to you to prepare for death and for that mercy which you will undoubtedly find in Heaven, but which you cannot expect here.
>
> The sentence of the court upon you is that you be hanged by the neck until you are dead, and that your body be buried within the precincts of the prison in which you shall have been confined before your execution, and may the Lord have mercy on your soul.

She was then removed to the condemned cell at Cardiff Prison, presumably because Swansea Prison did not have female facilities.

Cardiff City Council decided to draw up a petition for a reprieve, to be sent to the Home Secretary, Herbert Gladstone[1]. Alderman John Jenkins MP, promised to obtain a meeting with Gladstone to explain the council's position. As usual, especially in the case of a woman, public petitions were initiated for a reprieve. Willis's solicitor received 120 letters on the Monday prior to the hanging in support of a reprieve, including two from members of the coroner's jury, who thought that she was only guilty of manslaughter. Herbert Gladstone was unmoved by this agitation, and confirmed that the law would take its course on the Wednesday as planned.

Willis asked the governor of Cardiff Prison, Mr H.B. le Mesurier, if she could have a meeting with her former partner,

Mr Macpherson, which he allowed. Mr Macpherson was sent an urgent telegram telling him to come at once. They had their emotional meeting in the condemned cell where she gave him a lengthy letter. This letter was reported to be full of remorse and regrets, but stated that she was resigned to her fate and hoped God would forgive her. She also beseeched him to keep the details of her fate from their two daughters.

The gallows at Cardiff were housed in an execution shed in a small yard quite close to the main gate, totally hidden from view by high walls. On the Tuesday prior to the execution, the prison staff tested the drop. Henry Pierrepoint, and his brother and assistant, Thomas, tested it again upon their arrival at the prison in the early afternoon. Willis stood 5ft 2in. tall and weighed 145lb (rather overweight), her drop being calculated at 5ft 9in.

Late on the Tuesday evening, Willis asked the governor for another meeting with Mr Lloyd. Willis made a full confession to him in the condemned cell, in an interview lasting nearly half an hour (see above). She reportedly told him that she could not go to her death without a clear conscience and that she did indeed willfully murder the baby on the train back from Hengoed, between Llanishen and Cardiff. She told Mr Lloyd that a sudden temptation to kill the child came over her and that she couldn't resist it. She asked him to let the trial judge and jurors know of her confession so that they would not have the execution of an innocent woman on their consciences. The chaplain of Cardiff Prison, the Rev Arthur Pugh, then gave Willis the sacrament.

To avoid any contact with the group of seven men and one woman who were being released from the prison on the Wednesday morning at the end of their sentences, the governor brought forward their release to 7 am.

The execution had been set for 8 am on Wednesday, 14 August, 1907, which possibly was her 44th birthday. She was still an attractive woman, her blaze of golden hair glinting in the morning sunshine as she was led across the yard to the execution shed. This was remarked upon by Henry Pierrepoint in his diary. Present were the usual officials, including the undersheriff, Mr. T.T. Williams, the governor, Mr H.B. le Mesurier, the chaplain, Rev Arthur Pugh, and the prison surgeon, Mr J.D. Williams. As was usual with a female execution, the press was not admitted.

A large crowd had gathered outside the prison to witness the official notices of the execution being put up on the prison gates at around 8.30 am, the event being photographed by the press and a few of the onlookers.

She was the last 'baby farmer' to be hanged and the seventh person to be executed at Cardiff Prison, which had been opened in 1854.

4. The Search for 'Rhoda'

As has already been remarked upon, the dearth of material, including that in the death file, is extraordinary. These are the transcripts of three such file documents.

A letter dated 31 July 1907:

re-Leslie James alias Rhoda Willis
I beg to acknowledge receipt of your letter of the 29th instant and in reply to inform you that I have had careful enquiries made as to this woman's history and character prior to the commission the crime of which she now stands convicted and fined as follows.

In the year 1893 she came to Cardiff from Sunderland accompanied by her husband, Thomas Willis, a marine engineer, and a girl about six years of age whom she called Emma Willis.

They went to live in apartments with a Mrs Carew at number three Jubilee Terrace Grangetown in the city where two children (girls) were born to her during their residence in Cardiff Thomas Willis went to sea while serving as a second engineer on the steamship 'Dalmer' he contracted yellow fever at Santos, Brazil, and died in the early part of the year 1896.

About that time his relatives came from Sunderland to Cardiff, and for some reason which is not known to my informant, they claimed and took away the two younger children leaving Emma Willis, then about nine years of age with the prisoner.

Mrs Willis soon afterwards took a situation as housekeeper but eventually met and cohabited with a marine engineer named Gregor MacPherson at first in this city and afterwards at Bryn-Glas Road, Newport, Monmouth.

About the year 1903 she returned to Cardiff and then cohabited with Robert Carew, a blacksmith [a son of her former landlady] at different addresses up to the end of June 1906 when she went to lodge at number hundred and 91 Railway Street, East Moors. On 16 July 1906 she was arrested at that address on a charge of stealing money, a war medal and clasps, the property of the landlord of the house brought before the justices and sentenced to 1 calendar months hard labour in the name of Rhoda Willis.

After her release from prison she obtained the situation as housekeeper to David Evans, bootmaker, 55 George Street Pontypool Monmouth and did not again come under the notice of the police here until her arrest at 132 port assembler Road on the charge of child murder.

During her periodical residences in this city it has been ascertained that she was a woman of drunken habits and low moral character.

I have been unable so far to trace any of the prisoner's relatives but find that the girl Emma Willis has for the past five years been in domestic service with Mrs John Edward Bartlett at 257 Newport Road in this city. This lady speaks very highly of the girls character and states that at the present time she has been kept in ignorance of the prisoner's convictions.

The prisoner possesses photographs of Emma Willis and the other two girls but from what can be seen by them there does not appear to be any facial resemblances. I am
  Sir
your obedient servant
head constable.

A letter dated 3 August 1907:

re-Leslie James alias Rhoda Willis
With further reference to my letter of the 31st ultimo I beg to inform you that it is also been ascertained that the man referred to therein as Gregor MacPherson is Stewart R MacPherson of 19 Ursula Street Bootle. I am communicating with the Bootle police with a view to getting further particulars respecting the woman James.
  I am et cetera

A letter dated 8 August 1907:

re-Leslie James alias Rhoda Willis
With further reference to my letters that the 31st ultimo and third instant I beg to inform you that I have had Stewart R MacPherson seen by the Bootle police and he states as follows: 'I became acquainted with this woman in 1891. She was then known to me as Rhoda Willis, a married woman separated from her husband. I began cohabiting with her in 1896 and have resided with her in

Cardiff, Newport, Mon: and Bootle, from that time until 1901 when she was enticed away from me by my brother Gregor MacPherson who at that time was a chief engineer in one of Morel's steamers sailing from Cardiff. I have not heard from my brother since 1901 and do not know his present whereabouts.

Whilst I was cohabiting with her, three children were born, viz: – Stuart who died, Dorothy who would now be 10, and Bessie seven. They went with her in 1901. She was attentive to the house and children we were getting on comfortably together before my brother came on the scene. An adopted daughter named Emma also went with them to Cardiff in 1901 this girl was living with Willis when I first made her acquaintance. Emma is now about 20.'

I have made enquiries for the man Gregor MacPherson and ascertained that he left the employ of Messer's morale almost 18 months ago but up to the present no further trace of him can be obtained.

I am et cetera

Welsh census 1901:

'Rhoda McPherson
Age in 1901: 32
Estimated birth year: abt 1869
Relation: Wife
Spouse: McGregor McPherson
Where born: Sunderland
Household Members:
Name   Age
Mc Gregor McPherson   32
Rhoda McPherson 32
Dorothy McPherson 3
Emma Willis 14

We do not even know when she was born. According to her Sunderland marriage certificate, it was 1864; according to her Cardiff marriage certificate, 1867; and according to the census, 1869. It will be noted that, according to her confession, 'Around the age of 19 she met and later married Thomas Willis'. So, birth 1869 for first marriage?

The most probable reason for the second marriage was that she was not properly married the first time around. In the latter half of the nineteenth century, it was not possible to be married before the age of 21 without parental or magisterial permission. But she would have been 19 in July 1888, perhaps even 18 if the rumour regarding her birthday being the date of execution was true. It is most unlikely therefore that she was executed on her 44th birthday as the Home Office inquest papers stated. She was more likely to have been 38 or 39.

5. Who was 'Emma Willis'?

Exhaustive research through the records of England and Wales for births marriages and deaths, which commenced in the 1840s have revealed totally negative results. It has not been possible to discover an Emma born anywhere in England and Wales, searching under all the appropriate variations of the name she married under, or for that matter, a candidate for her putative 'deceased father', whether as brewer or publican. The records of the licensed Victuallers Association, a thriving organization over this period, yielded a blank.

There is no record of the birth of Emma Willis, her daughter, born the year before her first marriage, under her name in Sunderland or Newcastle. Emma Jr, however, believed she was the daughter of 'Rhoda' and Thomas Willis and told her descendants as much. According to the first police report, 'Emma' had a total of four living daughters: two by Thomas Willis and two by Stuart McGregor. They have disappeared, according to all official records of births, marriages and deaths. One is left with the conclusion that they were registered under different names or adopted. There is no usable photograph of Emma/Rhoda. The police photograph of 'Leslie James alias Rhoda Willis', taken when she was charged with murder, has faded over the years to an indecipherable blank.

However, Thomas Willis did not die of yellow fever abroad. It appears that he lived the rest of his life in Cardiff and must have walked out on Emma in or about 1896, possibly when she took up with their landlady's son, the blacksmith. He is not to be traced in the 1901 census, but obviously fell on hard times. The 1911 census finds him in Cardiff Workhouse, where he correctly describes himself as 'widower'. Thomas Robert Willis is documented throughout his life, save that he does not appear or easily identifiable in either the 1891 or 1901 census.

The Mercantile Marine Memorial for the First World War lists his death on board the SS *Frimaire*. He was drowned as a result of an attack by an enemy submarine on 15 March 1917, at the age of 57, while serving as the second engineer. He is recorded as the husband of Mary Ann Willis of 15 Louisa Street, Cardiff, in the docks area.

Hypothesis

There are only two Ernest Cameron Dalzells recorded as being alive in the UK during Mrs Willis's lifetime. Ernest Cameron Snr was born in 1854 in Birmingham. He married another Birmingham girl from the Dowler family in 1875. Her Christian name was Emma! Their only child, Ernest Cameron Dalzell Jr was born in 1876.

By 1881, Ernest Snr is calling himself a widower and living with his parents and junior. Sometime between 1876 and 1881, Emma Dalzell presumably died, but I cannot trace an entry in the registrar of deaths.

In the 1870s, divorce was very expensive and a preserve of the moneyed middle classes. It is therefore a possibility that Ernest and Emma agreed to go their separate ways. The result could be that Emma (nee Dowler) was entitled to call herself Emma Dalzell, but not as being single. The subsequent history of Ernest Snr may give some sort of explanation as to why the second marriage differs from the first in giving the full name of Ernest Cameron Dalzell as her father. By 1883, Ernest Snr had emigrated to America and remarried in 1886. The marriage produced two daughters: Elizabeth born in 1886 and Jessie, born in 1888. By 1900, he had prospered, with a jeweller's shop in Manhattan.

So, by their second marriage, the Willises could be reasonably sure that Emma's secret was safe, as Ernest was no longer to be found in the United Kingdom.

Our problem is the complete lack of evidence that a candidate spinster, Emma Dalzell, ever existed before the first marriage. Is it possible that Emma was born Emma Dowler? The chief drawback is that Emma Dowler was born in 1853, and therefore would have had to have been in her mid-40s when she produced the MacPherson children. But then her mother produced her last child in her mid-forties.

Another even more shaky hypothesis, without external evidence, is that Emma was indeed born in 1869, the illegitimate daughter of the 15-year-old Ernest.

Of course, one day, someone is going to find a gravestone for Emma Dowler.

6. Conclusion

Kate Webster (1849–1879) and Louie Calvert (1895–1926) lived fifty years apart, so it would be surprising if Calvert had ever heard of Webster and yet …

Both women commenced their public criminal career in their teens. They specialized in larceny, with prostitution on the side. They both used aliases: Kate Webster – Webster, Webb, Shannon, Lawless. Louie Calvert – Edith Thompson, Louise Jackson. They were both around 30 when they committed the violent murders for which they were convicted. They had known and lived with their victims for a matter of weeks and both victims were lonely widows. The motives for the murders were essentially theft. The victims were killed in their own homes. The method of murder was the same: battery, followed by strangulation.

Lengthy confessions and autobiographies, of dubious veracity, were made in the death cell. Webster was illiterate and made a series of statements to her solicitor. They both pretended to be married to 'captains' of superior status: Webster's was the Merchant Navy, Calvert's in the army.

At the time of their trial, they both had a single dependent son, of unascertained fatherhood, aged about 5, and to whom they were devoted.

E. O'Donnell, editor of the trial of Kate Webster in the *Notable British Trials*, and writing half a century after Webster's execution, observed:

'She was not merely savage, savage and shocking, but she had other attributes as well; attributes to which I shall refer later and which, in my opinion, are sufficient to place her outside any existing criminal and psychological category'.

Berry and Huggett, in their book *Daughters of Cain*, written in the 1950s, said of Calvert:

> Louie Calvert is the only woman of the nine executed since Edith Thompson in 1923 who can be called a criminal type. Many psychologists now prefer to believe that there is no such type, but there are nevertheless certain basic characteristics and tendencies which are usually evident ... Mrs Calvert's behaviour arose not only out of a situation but was part of her personality and mode of life.

From what we know of her, 'Rhoda Willis' led a messy and inventive double life without criminal acts, until the serious head injury in 1907. Her character then changed and she exhibited all the characteristics to be found in the lives of Kate Webster and Louie Calvert. Rapid changes of name, theft from an employer and murder of a baby for gain followed within a few months. It is clear that the accident changed her from a fantasist to a monster.

Agnes Norman was a wholesale killer for a period of two years. Where she differs is that she does not appear to have been a thief and was, so far as we can judge, cured of her killing mania.

So much of what I have discovered, however, is counterintuitive and flies in the face of popular conceptions: that such serial killers come from poverty-stricken and emotionally deprived origins, that they tend to come from 'bad families' where most of their close relatives have been in either serious criminal trouble, confined to mental institutions, or both.

In reality, Agnes Norman and Louie Calvert came from very similar backgrounds. Both Clipston and Gawthorpe were industrial villages, typical of their regions. Their respective fathers were skilled artisans in the main trade of the village and, so far as records go, neither of them were physically or emotionally deprived. In the case of Louie Calvert, the police report (supra) supports this. I have been unable to discover through the published criminal records that extend to 1892 any criminality in their parents' ancestry, or for their siblings.

We do not know much about the family background of Kate Webster. What we do know argues against destitution. Her uncle in the 1880s was a farmer in the most prosperous part of rural Ireland. Unfortunately, we know nothing about Emma Willis's background, but her voice was considered genteel, and there was speculation in the press that she had been a lady's maid at one time.

They all appear to be one-off psychopaths in their family setting. Certainly, the Norman and Gomersall families appear to have gone to great lengths to support their 'ugly ducklings'.

Epilogue

What follows is a broad, brush-stroke layman's guide to a very old question. Is there indeed a special criminal group to which these women might belong?

It was recognized early in the nineteenth century that there was such a category. In 1801, Philippe Pinel[1] used a phrase to describe people he recognized as having 'insanity without delirium'. Others lacking consciences, were described as people with a 'moral derangement'.

English psychiatrist James Prichard[2] described individuals whose moral judgement was absent or flawed, but whose intellectual judgement was intact, as suffering from 'moral insanity'. There were many labels for this blend of rational thought processes and depravity. Sociopath and psychopath entered into general use in the twentieth century.

What has been discovered is that there is a group of psychopaths called criminal psychopaths. This classification explicitly entails persistent criminal behaviour. It is important to emphasize that this group of psychopaths is the only group for which there is now neurobiological data to begin to get a preliminary idea of how the brain structure and function relates to antisocial behaviour. It is quite obvious that many of this group are available in prison for researchers. Other psychopaths are not available. Indeed, many of them are to be found among ruthless chief executives of important companies. They are not all murderers It is important to realize that criminal, psychopathic activity ranges from petty theft, particularly through fraudsters and confidence tricksters, through to the extremes of the serial killer. However, Kiehl and Judge Hoffman[3] estimated that over 90 per cent of adult male psychopaths in the US were in prison jail parole or probation.

Perhaps the easiest model to understand is the three aspect, or Triarchic, model, developed by Christopher Patrick[4]. His model attempts to make better sense of various descriptions of psychopathy that emphasize core features of the disorder. The components are disinhibition, boldness and meanness.

Disinhibition describes an inability to control impulses.

Boldness covers social dominance, emotional resiliency and venturesomeness.

Meanness is the aggressive behaviour used to obtain benefits without concern for victims.

As pointed out in the seminal textbook *Murderous Minds*, a person with brain-activity patterns identical to those seen in the brains of psychopaths may not be a psychopath. A person with genetic traits associated with violent behaviour may not be a psychopath. A person who was abused as a child, or who was exposed to violence, may not turn into a psychopath, but when these factors are combined in one person, watch out. All the ingredients for creating a psychopath are then present.

The most widely used evaluation system for criminal psychopathy is the Hare Psychopathy Checklist Revised, PCL-R[5]. Dr Robert Hare originally devised it over forty years ago. It has constantly been revised, the latest version having come out in 2003. The PCL-R rates each of twenty antisocial behaviour items of emotional and interpersonal traits on a three-point scale. The interview portion of the evaluation covers the subject's background, including such items as work and educational history, marital and family status, and criminal background. Because psychopaths lie frequently and easily, the information they provide must be confirmed by a review of the documents in the subject's case history.

When properly completed by a qualified professional, the PCL-R provides a total score that indicates how closely the test subject matches the 'perfect' score that a classic or prototypical psychopath would rate. Each of the twenty items is given a score of 0, 1, or 2, based on how well it applies to the subject being tested. A prototypical psychopath would receive a maximum score of 40, while someone with absolutely no psychopathic traits or tendencies, would receive a score of zero. We have sufficient information to attempt to apply the Hare Test to the three adults.

Scores:

Louie Calvert, 37

Kate Webster, 36

Rhoda Willis, 15

A score of 30 or above qualifies a person for a diagnosis of psychopathy. People with no criminal backgrounds normally score around 5. Many non-psychopathic criminal offenders score around 22.

Mrs Willis appears to be fairly normal. However, if we apply only those items of test relevant to her conduct after the head injury, a different type of picture emerges:

glib and superficial charm, 2

grandiose (exaggeratedly high) estimation of self, 2 (invention of Moneyed Background)

need for stimulation, 0
pathological lying, 2
cunning and manipulativeness, 2
lack of remorse or guilt, 1 (remorse only at day before execution)
shallowness (superficial emotional responsiveness), 2
parasitic lifestyle, 2
poor behavioral controls, 2
sexual promiscuity, 2
lack of realistic long-term goals, 2
impulsivity, 2
failure to accept responsibility for own actions, 2
criminal versatility, 1

The fourteen relevant attributes give a maximum score of 28. The new score for Mrs Willis is 24, a psychopathic score level.

Whilst one cannot apply the full range of the test to Agnes Norman, she scores 26 out of 30 for those parts applicable to her. From conviction onwards, however, she lives a blameless life, so far as one can tell. There are indications from the material that she might have got catharsis from the killing experience, as in this police report:

> Mr and Mrs Gardner went out at 8 ¼ p.m. and left their infant child James Alexander Gardner age 14 months in bed in charge of Agnes Norman at 8 ½ p.m. it cried, and as she was downstairs she went up to it and as she did not come down again, shortly after the Cook went up to the nursery and found her kneeling down by her bedside with her head upon her arm as though she was asleep.
>
> Attempted murder trial.
>
> Charles Parfitt: 'Ellen was on the bed when I first felt this on my mouth. She was lying on me across my back.'

I have only been able to trace one other parallel case.

Laura Humber, aged either 10 or 12, was charged in Wisconsin, USA, with the attempted murder of her parents and three sisters. It is alleged that she tortured to death three domestic animals and a dozen chickens. What is weird about this case was that it was almost entirely based on the evidence of her father, who called her a monster. Yet the 1905 census shows that she was living back at her own home with her mother father and siblings. She married, had a number of children, and earned herself several family trees in Ancestry.com, none of which mention any criminal activity at all. Is there a very rare form of killing mania that only persists through early adolescence and then disappears?

Over 150 years ago, a landmark industrial injury occurred[6]. On 13 September 1848, railroad worker, Phineas Gage, was tamping blasting powder into a hole, using a three-and-a-half-foot iron rod, when the powder exploded. The rod shot through Gage's skull, entering his left cheek and exiting through the top of his head.

Amazingly, Gage survived this massive injury. In fact, one observer reported that Gage was able to walk away from the accident, 'talking with composure and equanimity of the hole in his head.'

The long-term effects of Gage's accident, however, were devastating. Previously a polite and sociable gentleman, Gage became an antisocial, foul-mouthed, irresponsible, bad-mannered lout and unrepentant liar. According to his friends, he was 'no longer Gage'. He drifted from job to job, finally dying penniless.

While Gage's life was ruined, his unfortunate accident taught researchers about the critical role of the brain's frontal lobes, the area of Gage's brain injured by the iron bar that penetrated his skull, in controlling behaviour, emotions, and judgement. Later studies proved that injuries to the frontal lobes, or diseases that damage this brain area, can cause disinhibited behavior, poor judgment, and even antisocial or criminal behavior.

As *Crime Times*[7], an American publication linking brain dysfunction to psychopathic behaviour, remarked in a commemorative article:

> Antonio Damasio and colleagues, who have studied a dozen patients with frontal lobe damage similar to Gage's, say that the patients are incapable of planning for the future, and are deficient in judgment, reasoning ability, and 'moral insight'. Other research links frontal lobe dysfunction to aggression, alcoholism, and psychopathic criminality, and suggests that the deviant behavior seen in many children with Fetal Alcohol Syndrome may stem from damage to this brain area.

Brain tumours can have the same effect. An egg-sized brain tumor caused a man with no history of pedophilia to begin molesting children, according to a report presented in 2002[8] at the annual meeting of the American Neurological Association.

The 40-year-old man, a married teacher, had never exhibited abnormal sexual impulses. When he began visiting child pornography websites, visiting prostitutes, and making sexual advances to young children, his wife left him. Eventually, he was convicted of child molestation, and entered a treatment program for paedophiles. He continued to display inappropriate sexual behavior, and was expelled from a rehabilitation program after propositioning the women attending the program.

Shortly afterwards, the man visited a hospital complaining of headaches and telling hospital staff that he feared that he would rape his landlady. Doctors noted that he exhibited balance problems, had lost the ability to write or copy drawings, and showed a lack of concern when he urinated on himself.

At this point, doctors ordered an MRI scan, which showed a large tumour in the right orbitofrontal cortex. The tumour was removed, and the man successfully completed his therapy and returned home. When his aberrant sexual thoughts and behaviours began resurfacing later, an MRI scan showed that the tumour had returned. When it was removed, the man's behaviour again returned to normal.

Russell Swerdlow and Jeffrey Burns, the University of Virginia Medical School doctors who reported the man's case, say that the location of the tumour was critical, because it compromised the function of a brain region responsible for judgment, social behavior, and self-control.

'We're dealing with the neurology of morality here,' says Swerdlow.

Noting that the tumour caused few physical symptoms, he says, 'It's one of those areas where you could have a lot of damage and a doctor would never suspect something's wrong.'

Other crimes, including homicides, have also been linked to brain tumours. One of the most infamous cases was that of Charles Whitman, who killed fifteen students at the University of Texas by firing on them from the school's bell tower. An autopsy showed that Whitman had a tumour in his amygdala, a brain area involved in emotional reactions.

The limited studies of psychopaths with brain disorders, including fits, which disclose that damage to the brain, however caused, if it occurs in certain crucial areas of function or intra-brain communication, creates them. Studying the history of Mrs Willis, it is hard not to conclude that her serious 'head injury' caused her transformation from alcoholic, promiscuous housewife, into the violent and dishonest psychopathic baby farmer she became.

End Notes

I have compiled these notes with twin, sometimes conflicting objectives of ensuring that those interested can examine my sources, while avoiding prolixity and duplication. The basic sources of information for each of these women's stories and quotes from them will therefore be placed at the head of their section. The one general source throughout all parts of this book is Ancestry.com, the genealogical search engine. It is the first port of call for modern researchers into the lives of those who have lived since the first census of the British Isles in 1841. All the British censuses, until 1911, birth, marriages and deaths, serious criminal convictions before 1892, and much else, is now readably available. Ancestry.com is the source of factual information unless otherwise indicated. Each census I rely on can be found in the body of the text.

Introduction

1. A. Bellinger, *Dead Woman Walking: Executed Women in England and Wales 1900–1955.* (Ashgate Publishing, Dartmouth, 2000)
2. Home Office *144 series*, National Archives.
3. G.P. Troup, *The Home Office.* (Putnam, London, 1925)
4. Home Office *144/418438 Louie Calvert*, National Archives.
6. E. O'Donnell, *Notable British Trials*: 'Kate Webster'. (William Hodge, London & Edinburgh, 1925)

Part 1

'MFPO3/102' at the National Archives includes all newspaper reports and police reports quoted.
Old Bailey Proceedings Online (www.oldbaileyonline.org.): July1871 trial of AGNES NORMAN (15).

Chapter 4

1. HeritageCentre@met.pnn.police.uk *Records for Sargent Mullard*, e-mail to author, 16 May16 2016.

Part 2

Home Office *144/418438 Louie Calvert*, National Archives. All quotes from the exercise book are prefaced by page numbers and retain original spelling and punctuation.

Chapter 1

1. R. Huggett and P. Berry, *Daughters of Cain*. (George Allen & Unwin, London, 1956)
2. H. Mankell, *Before the Frost* (English Translation). (The New Press, New York & London, 2005)
3. 1914–1918 War Service and Pension Records, National Archives.

Chapter 4

1. Kew archives 1910. Pris.Com 7.561.
2. Kew archives 1910. Pris.Com 7.587.

Chapter 9

1. A compilation from the following sources:
   Police News, Thursday, 4 February 1926
   Police News, Thursday, 8 April 1926
   Sheffield Daily Telegraph, 28 January 1926
   Manchester Guardian, 26 February 1926
   C.L. Scott, *Unsolved Murders in South Yorkshire*. (Warncliffe, Barnsley, 2013)

Part 3

1. 'HO144/82518' Kate Webster.
2. E. O'Donnell, *Notable British Trials*: 'Kate Webster'. (William Hodge, London & Edinburgh, 1925)

Chapter 1

1. Law Society, England and Wales Archives.

Chapter 2

1. *Wikipedia* Elliott O'Donnell.

Chapter 4

1. E. O'Donnell, *Notable British Trials*: 'Kate Webster'. (William Hodge, London & Edinburgh, 1925)
2. E. O'Donnell, *Great Thames Mysteries*. (Selwyn and Blunt, London, 1929)
3. M.J. Trow, *The Thames Torso Murders*. (Warncliffe, Barnsley, 2012)

Part 4

'HO144/155396' Leslie James.

Chapter 1

1. *Western Daily Mail*, 15 August 1907, for the whole incident.

Chapter 2

1. *Evening Express*, 23 July 1907.
2. *The Cambrian*, 26 July 1907.

Chapter 3
1. *Western Daily Mail*, 1 August 1907 onwards for this narrative.

Epilogue
Chapter 1
1. B. Mackler, (Franklin Watts Inc., 1969)
2. J. *Prichard, A Treatise on Insanity and Other Disorders Affecting the Mind.* (Sherwood, Gilbert, and Piper, London, 1835)
3. K.A. Kiehl, *The Psychopath Whisperer: The Science of Those Without Conscience.* (Crown Publishers, New York, 2014)
4. D.A. Haycock, *Murderous Minds.* (Pegasus Books, 2014)
5. R.D. Hare, *Without Conscience* New York, London, (The Guilford Press, London, 2002)
6. S. Baron-Cohen, *Zero Degrees of Empathy.* (Allan Lane, London, 2011)
7. *Crime Times* Vol.4, No.4, 1998.
8. J.M. Burns, *Arch. Neurological,* Vol. 60, 2003.

Index